The Three P's of People Development

A Manager's Guide to Motivating, Rewarding and Advancing Your Team

Marvin D. Glover

GMG Management Group LLC

Table of Contents

PREFACE

Leaders often think that fair pay alone will keep employees motivated and performing well. I used to believe this early in my leadership career. However, I eventually realized that this wasn't the full picture. I observed employees who met goals, delivered results, and contributed positively to their teams, yet they still became discouraged. Some decided to leave the organization despite strong performance and competitive pay; something was missing.

What prompted me to reflect on what truly motivates people? I observed individuals who had achieved their sales targets, yet the process was difficult and draining. Instead of feeling proud or energized, they looked frustrated and disengaged. The usual ideas of motivation, hard work, reaching goals, and earning money didn't quite align with what I saw. Something deeper was happening behind the scenes of organizational success. As I continued to observe and study my leadership and teams, additional patterns emerged. I had conducted one-on-one meetings with two managers, both of whom were seeking promotions. My first assumption was that their reasons were similar, but their motivations were very different. One sought financial gain, while the other wanted more responsibility and influence. These insights revealed a key truth: leaders often believe they understand what motivates their staff, but they are mostly guessing. When their guesses are wrong, they tend to use the wrong solutions.

Organizations often rely on directive leadership, which involves giving orders without truly understanding what motivates employees. While this approach may secure immediate compliance, it often fails to build lasting engagement. Over time, I've seen a troubling trend: top performers leaving organizations not for a lack of skill, but because they lack proper guidance and authentic leadership.

In the absence of honest communication and intentional development, capable team members can become disengaged and lose their sense of purpose.

Through these experiences, I began to ask a simple yet powerful question: What truly motivates people at work?

Over more than thirty years in leadership and management roles, the answer slowly became clearer. My career has taken me through various environments, from serving in the United States Army to leading teams in the private sector. Each setting was different, yet the same leadership challenge kept coming up: leaders struggled to understand what truly motivated the individuals they were responsible for developing.

During this period, one of the most valuable lessons I learned was the importance of genuine conversation. Leadership isn't based on assumptions; it's built on clear communication. By engaging in honest discussions with team members, I gained a better understanding of what individuals prioritize most in their work.

These conversations showed that people were often motivated by different reasons, even when they held similar roles within the same organization. Eventually, a clear pattern emerged.

Most motivational challenges stem from three main factors: Praise, Pay, and Position.

Some individuals are motivated by praise, recognition that their efforts are appreciated and their contributions are valued. Others are motivated by pay, the monetary rewards that reflect the results they achieve. Still, others are motivated by position, the chance to grow, advance, and assume greater responsibilities within an organization.

When leaders identify the most important motivational driver for an individual, their leadership quality improves markedly. Conversations deepen, and development initiatives become more targeted. As a result, the workplace becomes a space where people feel genuinely understood rather than just managed.

I first introduced this to interviewers, explaining the three motivational drivers. This is a simple way leadership can develop teams. After applying the Three P's of People Development Model in real leadership situations, especially while managing multiple units, the results became clearer. When leaders focused on understanding these motivational drivers, interactions improved, productivity increased, and teams became more aligned.

The Three P's of People Development offers leaders three simple, straightforward perspectives for diagnosing motivation. Instead of making assumptions, leaders can ask more insightful questions and observe team members' cues more closely. Although each driver is significant on its own, together they provide a more comprehensive view of what drives people. These three factors often interact to shape how individuals perceive their work and growth opportunities.

I wrote this book to provide something simple and tangible that leaders can continually refer to as they develop their teams. The Three P's of People Development is more than a concept: it's a practical approach to understanding people and leading them more effectively. I hope that leaders who read this book will start diagnosing their teams differently, looking beyond surface-level solutions and focusing on what truly drives engagement and growth.

When leaders learn to recognize these motivational drivers, they can begin unlocking new opportunities. Instead of losing talented individuals, you can retain and promote them from within. Leaders who develop people intentionally, not by assumption, achieve internal promotions and consistently high retention as successful outcomes.

This book is for growth-focused leaders, eager to move beyond conventional management and embrace purposeful leadership. Visionary leaders who see the broader scope of organizational success will recognize that nurturing people isn't merely a duty; it's one of their most effective tools.

If you consistently apply the principles outlined in this book, you may observe a notable change within your team. Productivity tends to increase, not only because expectations become clearer, but also because team members feel truly understood and appreciated. Leadership discussions will increasingly focus on development, and employees will begin to see a future for themselves within their organizations.

Ultimately, every individual is motivated by a specific driver. The Three P's of People Development provides a simple structure for identifying these drivers. A leader's challenge is not just the day-to-day management of their team but also understanding them.

As you read the upcoming chapters, I encourage you to reflect on your own leadership experiences, conversations with team members, and the impact motivation has on performance. I hope that you might find that the most powerful leadership lessons are often the simplest, sometimes summarized in just three words: Praise, Pay, Position.

INTRODUCTION

When a team loses motivation, many leaders assume external factors such as market pressures, staffing shortages, or generational gaps are to blame. However, performance typically deteriorates from within the team, shaped by how people are led, motivated, and developed. Employees don't leave companies; they leave because of poor or unintentional leadership.

Most managers aren't ineffective because they lack effort; they struggle because they try to motivate everyone the same way. They assume that compensation drives performance, encouragement builds loyalty, or that promotion solves engagement. None of that is true. Every individual is primarily motivated by one of three drivers: Praise, Pay, or Position. Some employees seek recognition. Others desire financial growth. Some want advancement and authority. When leaders treat everyone equally but not individually, engagement declines, turnover increases, and performance stalls. It's the leader's job to identify which driver motivates each person.

People development is a leadership skill, not a personality trait. Modern leadership requires clarity, consistency, and follow-through. High-performing teams rely on clear, reinforced expectations that align with what motivates each person. When leaders connect motivation to standards, employees understand what success looks like and how to achieve it. This alignment reduces confusion, boosts accountability, and improves retention.

Consider a familiar moment: you publicly praise one employee for exceptional work, and another immediately questions the fairness of the recognition. The issue isn't praise; it's the assumption that everyone values recognition the same way. A common leadership mistake is treating everyone the same rather than leading based on what motivates them. Motivation, like development, is a matter of discipline. Effective managers create systems that reinforce expectations, reward the right behaviors, and recognize the individual drivers that influence performance.

This book offers a straightforward, practical leadership model for diagnosing and aligning motivation. Which of the Three P's- Praise, Pay, or Position drives an individual? It also guides leaders in intentionally fostering growth and avoiding emotional, random, or reactive approaches. The book helps leaders create environments where standards are clear, motivation aligns with goals, and development is ongoing.

To begin with, leaders need to reflect carefully.

Who on your team responds best to public praise, and who prefers private feedback?

What would change if development conversations occurred every month?

What kind of value exchange would justify a pay raise within your current budget?

Leadership excellence is not accidental. It is built through disciplined clarity, intentional motivation, and the ability to develop people individually long before performance issues or turnover force the conversation.

PART I - FOUNDATIONS

UNDERSTANDING THE DRIVERS OF MOTIVATION

Chapter 1

The Motivation Fallacy

The Resignation That Didn't Make Sense

It was Monday morning, 8:17 a.m., when a leader received an unexpected email titled "Thank You." The message contained only two words, with no further details. The resignation came as a shock, considering that three months earlier, the employee had received a pay raise, positive performance reviews, bonuses, and flexible schedules. By all Key Performance Indicators (KPIs), this person should have stayed.

The leader's immediate reaction was: "After everything we've done?" This sentiment reveals a common leadership problem. Leaders often confuse effort with alignment. They mistakenly believe that by increasing pay, offering praise, or granting flexibility, they have effectively addressed motivation. But motivation is not about what leaders give. It is about what individuals value most. And those are rarely the same.

The Dangerous Assumption

The dangerous assumption sits quietly beneath most organizational decisions. Most organizations operate under a flawed belief: "If we pay people more, they will stay." Pay motivates, but it's not always the primary driver. Employees are often motivated by recognition, financial growth, advancement, and authority. When leaders apply the wrong driver, employees disengage, and their performance becomes unstable, and culture suffers. The fallacy of motivation is believing that one strategy fits all. It never does.

The problem is not that pay is unimportant. The problem is that pay is often treated as a universal solution. When leaders default to compensation, they skip diagnosis. They assume the problem is financial when the real issue is often visibility, progression, or influence.

A praise-driven employee may accept less pay if they feel seen and reinforced. A pay-driven employee may leave even in a strong culture if the value exchange feels unclear. A position-driven employee may outperform everyone on the team and still leave if they cannot see a future. The Three P's do not compete; they clarify a person's motivation.

When leaders apply the wrong driver, they may see a temporary lift; then a sharper drop. Raises offer short-term relief but do not address invisibility. Titles create short-term excitement but do not resolve perceived undervaluation. Compliments boost morale in the short term but do not replace advancement. Over time, misalignment produces the same outcomes: inconsistent effort, quiet disengagement, and avoidable turnover.

Before you change pay, expand responsibility, or increase recognition, ask one question: Which driver is actually being challenged – Praise, Pay, or Position?

The next section shows what happens when leaders guess and act anyway.

Applying the Wrong Driver

A regional director takes over a department with high turnover. Exit interviews indicated employees were unhappy with pay. The director's quick response was to raise salaries, adjust bonuses, and improve benefits for all staff.

For three months, employee morale improved, but by the sixth month, performance began to decline because the response targeted the wrong driver.

After one-on-one meetings, patterns emerged. Senior analysts asked about promotion pathways; high performers requested cross-functional opportunities; and team leads requested decision-making authority.

Most of the turnover risk was tied to position-related factors rather than pay. The director misidentified the primary driver. Financial incentives and salary increases offer only short-term fix and failed to promote long-term engagement. Senior analysts valued career growth opportunities more than just higher pay.

By focusing only on compensation growth rather than positional advancement, the director misidentified the primary driver, resulting in short-term relief. When leaders misidentify a position-driven employee as pay-driven, they unintentionally trigger employee disengagement. Raises can buy time, but they can't achieve true alignment. Without alignment, even high performers might begin to underperform.

This is the pattern behind most retention failures. Leaders respond to the first complaint they hear, apply the most convenient fix, and assume the issue is resolved. But when the wrong driver is applied, the employee may become quieter, not because they are satisfied, but because they realize leadership is not seeing the real issue.

Using pay to solve a position problem provides short-term relief and leads to long-term stagnation. Using position to solve a praise problem increases responsibility while the need for reinforcement remains unmet. Using praise to solve a pay problem builds goodwill, but it cannot repair a broken value exchange. The root issue is not generosity; it is misdiagnosis.

To correct this, leaders must understand why they guess in the first place – what biases and habits drive misdiagnosis. Those motivational factors can be predictable.

Pillar: Position

When leaders misidentify position-driven employees as pay-driven, they inadvertently trigger disengagement.

Motivational Factors

1. Projection-Value Projection: Leaders may assume others are motivated by what motivates them, defaulting to pay because it, to praise because they value recognition, or to promotion because they value it.

2. Simplicity Bias-simplicity replaces strategy: It is often easier for leaders to adjust compensation than to redesign advancement pathways, to promote than to develop, and to say "good job" than to build structured recognition programs.

3. Emotional Response-quick fixes: When high performers express frustration, many leaders' quick emotional responses tend to be a "let's fix it" approach, offering quick fixes like raises or bonuses without properly diagnosing the underlying cause of the misalignment.

Scenario: The Wrong Fix - Imagine This Situation

Imagine a high-performing supervisor, uncertain about their future within the organization, approaches you and says, "I'm not sure I see my future here."

What do you do? The instinctive reaction many leaders have is to offer raises, bonuses, or additional perks. But the right response is not to default to compensation but to identify the true motivator. When leaders rush to offer financial solutions, they often miss the underlying driver shaping performance, engagement, and retention. Compensation may satisfy, but it does not reveal what a person is truly working toward.

A more effective approach is to determine the true motivator behind the employee's concerns. Instead of defaulting to compensation, a leader should ask: "What does your ideal future here look like?" This question can reveal whether the individual's motivations are tied to praise, pay, or position. Only by identifying the real motivator, praise, pay, or position, can a leader respond accurately rather than by assumption.

The Three P's Diagnostic Lens

Moving forward, every leadership decision must pass through one filter: What primarily motivates this person?

This lens is not a personality test. It is a leadership discipline. It forces you to separate what you value from what the employee is signaling, and it prevents you from using the wrong solution simply because it is the easiest to deliver.

1. **Observe** what they repeat: questions they ask, what frustrates them, and what they protect.
2. **Confirm** in conversation: ask one clarifying question that reveals what "progress" means to them.
3. **Apply** one targeted adjustment: reinforce, reward, or expand responsibility—then watch the response.

Use the Three P's as a sorting mechanism. If you cannot answer these questions, you are not ready to intervene:

- **Praise:** Which standard do they want affirmed, and where do they feel unseen?
- **Pay:** What evidence would convince them the value exchange is fair and progressing?
- **Position:** What does the next level look like, and what path do they believe is blocked?

Once the driver is clear, leadership becomes precise:

The Three P's:

- **Praise** – Recognition and reinforcement of contributions
- **Pay** – Compensation and measurable reward
- **Position** – Advancement and influence opportunities

By understanding these three P's, leaders can foster a work environment that truly engages employees and aligns with their motivational drivers.

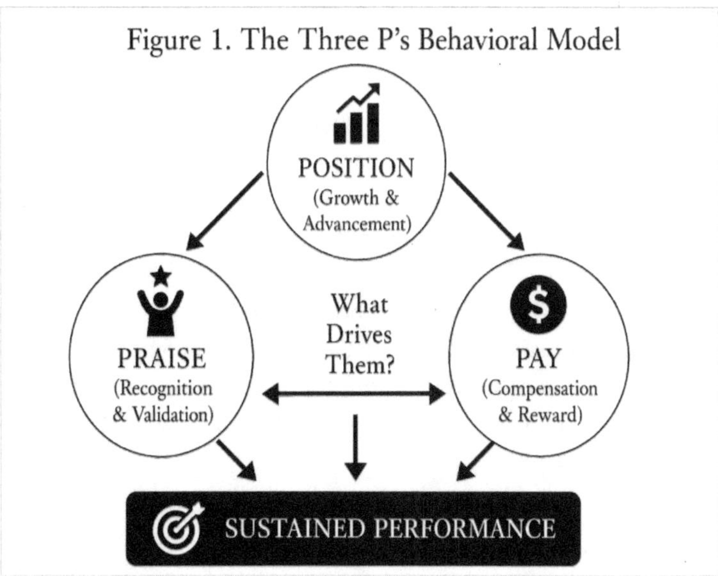

Figure 1. The Three P's Behavioral Model

Most individuals value all three, but one dominates. That single driver shapes how they engage, respond, and grow. Your job is not to guess which one it is. Your job is to observe what they respond to, what they repeat, and what they protect, because their dominant motivator is always revealed in their actions before it is expressed verbally.

Motivational Drivers

- Praise-driven employees frequently seek feedback, respond strongly to recognition, desire acknowledgment of performance, and perform well in environments where performance is visible.

Warning Sign: If unrecognized, they disengage quietly.

- Pay-driven employees track compensation benchmarks, frequently ask about bonus structures, compare pay with peers, and associate success with earnings.

Warning Sign: If compensation lacks clarity, they reduce engagement to a simple exchange of effort for compensation.

- Position-driven employees ask about career advancement opportunities, seek leadership opportunities, greater responsibility, and measure progress by authority, title and position.

Warning Sign: If growth pathways are unclear, employees look externally.

The Misunderstood High Performer

A hospitality senior executive managed a property with an exceptional assistant manager. The individual regularly exceeded revenue targets and maintained strong guest satisfaction metrics. The senior executive assumed financial incentives were the motivator and increased the performance bonus.

Six months later, the assistant manager resigned to accept a lateral position at another company. In the exit conversation, the manager said, “I wanted leadership exposure. I didn’t need more money.” The executive later admitted: “I never asked what he wanted long term.”

Pillar: Position

When position aspirations go unasked and unmet, pay incentives increase output but not commitment.

Misinterpretation Costs Talent

When leadership misinterprets drivers' praise, pay, or position, their responses feel out of sync, prompting employees to question whether their contributions are understood or valued.

The Cost of Misalignment

When motivations are misaligned, businesses face a range of problems: higher turnover, less discretionary effort, declining innovation, cultural instability, and leadership burnout. These issues may not be immediately apparent. Replacing a middle manager often costs more than their annual salary. The loss of a future executive is invaluable.

Misalignment is costly because it is rarely isolated. When praise is missing, high performers stop feeling seen, and standards erode. When pay is unclear or inconsistent, the value exchange becomes questionable, and effort turns transactional. When position is vague, ambition shifts toward external exploration. Each failure mode creates a distinct form of erosion, but they all produce the same outcome: reduced commitment, followed by reduced performance.

The most costly part is that leaders often misidentify the driver. Turnover is a lagging indicator. The earlier indicators are quieter: fewer stretch efforts, less initiative, reduced ownership, and a noticeable shift toward "just enough." Misalignment does not always look like conflict; it looks like compliance without commitment.

Misalignment also damages credibility. When leaders respond with the wrong driver such as more praise when pay is the issue, more pay when growth is the issue or more responsibility when reinforcement is the issue, employees stop believing leadership understands them. That doubt becomes culture drift; standards become inconsistent, fairness becomes a rumor, and "future" becomes an external concept. The reflection audit below is designed to surface where that drift is already forming.

Reflection Audit – Chapter 1

1. Have you increased compensation without defining performance measures?
2. Have you been giving praise that isn't tied to a specific outcome?
3. Have you given promotions based on tenure rather than performance readiness?
4. Which of the top three performers have you formally asked about their developmental and long-term goals?

Your answers to these questions can determine if you are operating under the fallacy of motivation.

Leadership Shift

Effective leaders do not react; they observe. They do not apply blanket solutions; they implement precise drivers. They recognize that motivation isn't about generosity; it's about alignment. Alignment starts with awareness: awareness of patterns, signals, and what everyone responds to.

Incorrectly diagnosing motivation leads to misguided leadership. When leaders assume rather than diagnose, they reward the wrong behaviors, reinforce the wrong drivers, and focus on the wrong motivator. The result isn't immediate failure but a slow decline in engagement, trust, and retention. Consequently, performance becomes unpredictable because the leadership response is misaligned.

This chapter lays a foundation: before praise, pay, or position can be used effectively, leaders must first understand what motivates behavior. Diagnosis is essential; it is the prerequisite. Without it, even well-meaning leadership becomes noise. With it, leadership becomes precise, repeatable, and effective. The following chapters build on this discipline. When leaders accurately diagnose, the strategy succeeds.

Misreading the driver – raise, Pay, or Position-doesn't just miss the moment; it costs talent.

Chapter 2 explores why good managers lose good people.

- **Invisible disengagement**
- **Cultural blind spots**
- **Early warning signs**
- **The slow erosion of loyalty**

Chapter 2

Why Good Managers Lose Good People

The Slow Exit No One Notices

Resignations rarely start with a single email; they typically develop over months. Disengagement isn't sudden, it happens gradually. A high performer stops volunteering for developmental assignments. They speak less in meetings. They complete tasks, without taking initiative. They are still present, but already detaching.

The tragedy isn't that good managers lose good people. The tragedy is that they often never realize it is happening.

The Myth of the "Good Manager"

Most managers believe they are good managers; they meet performance targets, avoid conflict, treat people respectfully, and pay fairly. These are baseline standards, not development strategies. A manager can be fair and still fail to develop others. They can be respectful and still misalign motivation. They can be competent and still lose talent. Being "good" is not enough.

Retention Risk Scenario – The Quiet Decline

A district manager oversaw six retail locations. One store consistently outperformed the others in revenue. The store manager was disciplined, organized, and steady.

The district manager believed, "She's solid. She doesn't need much." Over the next year, revenue plateaued, engagement scores dipped, and two strong assistant managers transferred.

The district manager finally scheduled a one-on-one. She asked, "Is everything okay?" The store manager responded calmly, "I'm fine." Three months later, she accepted a position elsewhere.

Exit interview insights revealed that she had informally asked about multi-unit development; no clear pathway was provided, and she interpreted the silence as a lack of investment. The district manager later reflected, "I thought stability meant satisfaction."

It didn't. It meant stagnation. What appeared to be steadiness was a quiet plateau, with the store manager holding their position not because they were fulfilled, but because nothing was changing. While leaders often interpret consistency as contentment, high performers interpret it as a ceiling. Stability without progression signals that growth has stalled, and once that realization sets in, commitment begins to loosen in subtle yet decisive ways.

Pillar: Position

Position-driven retention requires clear advancement pathways, because stability without progression is perceived as a ceiling, leading to disengagement and exit.

The Three Silent Killers of Retention

1. ***Invisibility:*** High performers want their work to matter. When effort goes unseen, loyalty erodes, and praise-driven individuals suffer first. Their motivation is tied to visibility — not attention-seeking, but acknowledgment that their contribution has weight, impact, and meaning. When that acknowledgment disappears, even subtly, their engagement begins to fracture.

2. ***Ceiling Perception:*** Position-driven employee motivation is rooted in growth, authority, and advancement. When opportunities stagnate, potential is overlooked, or leadership roles are assigned without a clear rationale, they disengage quietly but decisively. They stop growing, stop initiating, and eventually stop believing the organization can meet their ambition. If a position driven employee cannot see advancement, they assume it does not exist. Ambiguity creates exit planning.

3. ***Compensation stall:*** Pay-driven employees' loyalty is tied to financial growth, equity, and the tangible exchange of effort for reward. When compensation stalls, raises feel arbitrary, or their contribution outpaces their pay, frustration replaces commitment.

They may still perform, but the emotional contract is broken. If pay-driven employees perceive their compensation as unclear, inconsistent, or capped without explanation, they consider alternatives. Uncertainty prompts exploration.

Scenario: The Missed Signal

Imagine a team member saying: "I've been thinking about expanding my responsibilities." That statement carries insight into the team member's true driver.

It may mean:

- They want growth (Position)
- They want increased compensation (Pay)
- They want recognition for capability (Praise)

Your response determines whether they stay.

The wrong response is, "We'll see what happens next year," while the strategic response is, "Let's define what expanded responsibility looks like and how readiness is measured."

Ambiguity causes disengagement, while clarity builds commitment. When expectations are unclear, employees tend to pull back in subtle, quiet ways that often go unnoticed. But when direction, standards, and motivation are clearly communicated, commitment increases, and performance becomes more consistent.

The Erosion Model

Retention does not collapse overnight. It erodes in stages.

1. Stage 1: Frustration
2. Stage 2: Silence
3. Stage 3: Emotional Withdrawal
4. Stage 4: External Exploration
5. Stage 5: Resignation

Most leaders only recognize Stage 5.

Effective leaders observe Stage 1.

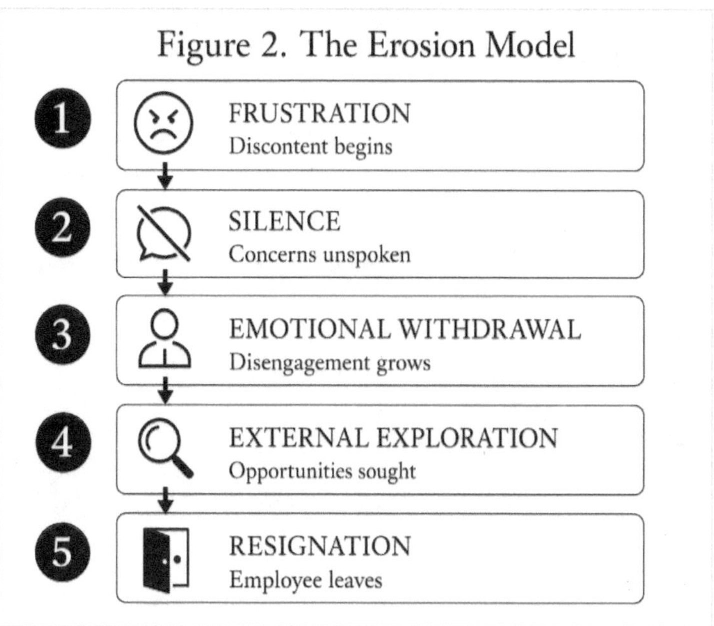

The High-Potential Exit

A financial services firm identified a junior analyst as high potential. Performance ratings were top-tier and bonuses were competitive. However, the analyst repeatedly sought greater exposure to strategic work.

Responses were polite but vague. *"We'll get you there eventually."* Eventually never came. After two years, the analyst accepted an offer from a competitor, with the same pay and title but a defined leadership development track.

The desire for growth, authority, and advancement which is central to a position-driven individual went unnoticed. While the organization believed that compensation, praise, and opportunity were enough, the analyst was waiting for something else: a clear path to advancement. The firm lost not just an employee but a future executive.

Position was the driver, but it was never acknowledged. What appeared to be a sudden decision was simply the final step in a progression that had been unfolding for months.

Pillar: Position

When advancement pathways remain unclear, position-driven talent interprets silence as a ceiling.

Why Managers Avoid Development Conversations

Many managers hesitate to discuss growth for three reasons:

1. They fear promising what they cannot deliver.
2. They lack structured pathways.
3. They are uncomfortable discussing ambition.

But avoiding the conversation does not prevent departure; it accelerates it.

Diagnostic Tool – Early Warning Indicators

Ask yourself:

- Who has recently become quieter?
- Who has stopped seeking feedback?
- Who has reduced discretionary effort?
- Who has started comparing compensation externally?
- Who has asked about advancement more than once?

These are not complaints, they are data. Each statement, concern, or pattern signals praise, pay, or position. What may seem like frustration is often an early indicator of misalignment, unmet motivators, or structural gaps that leadership has not yet identified or addressed. When leaders fail to identify motivators, they miss the insights they contain. However, when they treat them as data, actionable information, they gain visibility into what is working, what is failing, and what requires intervention before talent is lost.

Leadership Dialogue Example

Employee said, "I've been here a while, and I'm just trying to understand what growth looks like." The manager responded reactively, saying, "Let's focus on your current role." A strategic manager, however, would respond by saying, "That's a fair question. Let's map your growth in measurable stages and define readiness criteria." The second response turns uncertainty into structure.

The Cultural Cost of Losing Good People

When high performers leave, standards decline, culture weakens, remaining employees question leadership, and trust erodes subtly. The impact is rarely sudden or loud; it unfolds quietly within the team's daily rhythm. The absence of a high performer creates gaps in execution, accountability, and morale that others sense long before leadership recognizes the long-term cost. Retention is not just about avoiding vacancies. It is about protecting culture, and preserving the expectations, energy, and excellence that high performers anchor.

Reflection Audit – Chapter 2

1. Who on your team may be in Stage 2 (Silence)?

2. Have you clearly defined advancement readiness criteria?

3. Does your compensation structure reward measurable value?

4. Are you relying on performance metrics instead of engagement indicators?

5. If your only retention strategy is "pay well," you are vulnerable.

Leadership Shift

Good managers maintain operations. Great leaders develop people. The difference is not effort; it is intention. Operations keep the organization running, but development keeps it moving forward. When leaders treat retention as a result rather than a strategy, they notice disengagement too late and resort to generic fixes.

Retention erosion usually begins with misalignment, praise becomes inconsistent, pay becomes unclear, or position becomes invisible. Leaders misinterpret early signals as attitude, burnout, or "normal turnover" because performance remains intact. But silence, reduced initiative, and withdrawal are not personality traits; they are data. When a leader ignores the data, the employee does not become more patient. They become more prepared to leave.

The leadership shift is to intervene earlier and more accurately: diagnose which driver is being challenged, then respond with the right driver. Great leaders do not wait for a resignation to start the conversation; they build a rhythm of development that makes the future measurable. Chapter 3 builds that diagnostic system.

Good managers maintain operations, while great leaders develop people.

Chapter 1 revealed the illusion.

Chapter 2 revealed the erosion.

Chapter 3 builds the system.

Chapter 3

Understanding What Drives Behavior

Can't Lead What You Don't Understand

Many leaders try to motivate their teams without first understanding them. They reward before observing, promote without evaluating, and compensate without measuring. Effective leadership is not reactive; it is diagnostic. When leaders rush to fix problems, offer incentives, or promote without understanding what truly motivates people, they end up with solutions that miss the mark and don't last. The order is important: observation must come before action, and insight must come before response. Only through proper observation can leaders identify the motivator that determines whether engagement grows stronger or weaker.

Reactive Leadership

Reactive leadership responds quickly without fully understanding the situation, basing actions on immediate observations. It rewards before it observes, promotes before it evaluates, and compensates before it measures. It assumes that action itself creates progress. But action without insight leads to misalignment. Employees feel managed, not understood. Motivation becomes inconsistent, and engagement becomes unpredictable. Turnover is often a surprise rather than a preventable pattern.

Diagnostic Leadership

Diagnostic leadership, on the other hand, responds intentionally and is rooted in clarity; it influences outcomes by uncovering the deeper causes of behavior. It recognizes that leadership is a discipline of interpretation. It observes patterns, listens for what goes unsaid, and considers the drivers, such as praise, pay, or position, that influence performance long before results appear. Diagnostic leaders don't rush to fix issues; they seek to understand first. They know that delivering the right intervention at the right time builds trust, strengthens commitment, and prevents disengagement.

Why the Contrast Matters

While reactive leaders respond to what they see in the moment, diagnostic leaders act on what they understand, focusing not only on behavior but also on the motivations that influence it.

This contrast matters because leadership isn't judged by how quickly a leader responds but by how accurately they do so. Reactive leadership offers temporary relief, while diagnostic leadership promotes long-term alignment. Reactive leadership treats everyone the same, whereas diagnostic leadership recognizes each motivator as unique. In environments where retention, culture, and performance depend on understanding people, diagnostic leadership makes the difference between losing talent and developing it.

Before you give praise, pay, or a position, you must answer one question: *What is this person primarily driven by?*

Without that answer, every action is guesswork.

Behavior is a Clue, Not a Complaint

Employees rarely reveal their motivational drivers directly; they show them through their actions. A leader who listens only to words will miss them, but a leader who studies patterns will see them clearly. Motivation is revealed through repeated questions, emotional reactions, triggers of frustration, what employees celebrate, and what they complain about. Patterns never lie.

Leaders often mislabel these signals as attitude, entitlement, or negativity. But behavior is rarely random. It is usually an adaptive response to a perceived gap in reinforcement, value exchange, or growth visibility. When you treat a signal like a complaint, you respond defensively. When you treat it like data, you respond diagnostically.

That is why Table 1 matters. It translates common statements and repeated behaviors into the most likely driver behind them. "No one notices the work we do" is usually a praise signal. "I'm not sure this is worth it anymore" often points to pay alignment and value exchange. "What does growth look like here?" is typically a position signal; an attempt to confirm whether a future exists inside the organization.

Use the table as a first-pass filter, not a final diagnosis. Listen for what is repeated, note what triggers frustration, and then confirm with one clarifying question before you intervene. The goal is precision: apply the right driver early, while engagement is still recoverable.

Table 1 provides a quick way to translate what you are seeing and hearing into a working hypothesis about the dominant driver.

Table 1. The Three P's Behavioral Matrix

Behavior Observed	Likely Motivation (P)	Leadership Response	Development Strategy
Seeks recognition, responds to praise	Praise	Provide specific, timely recognition	Reinforce behaviors tied to performance
Focused on compensation, asks about pay	Pay	Link performance to rewards	Set measurable performance targets
Asks about advancement, growth opportunities	Position	Assign stretch responsibilities	Build leadership readiness

Misidentified motivation leads to misapplied leadership. *Example:*

Table 2. Misidentified Motivation

Manager Action	Employee Driver	Result
Raise given	Position	Employee remains dissatisfied
Promotion offered	Pay	Employee disengaged
Recognition given	Pay	No performance change

Every employee is driven by one dominant motivational driver. For a praise-dominant individual, recognition fuels effort. For a pay-dominant individual, financial growth fuels commitment. For a position-dominant individual, advancement fuels loyalty. The leader's job is not to label permanently; it is to identify the current dominant driver. Drivers can evolve with career stage, shifting as responsibilities, aspirations, and personal priorities change.

Leadership Diagnostic Questions

Managers can determine the dominant "P" by asking:

Praise-Driven Employee:

- "Do they respond strongly to recognition?"
- "Does appreciation increase performance?"
- "Do they seek validation from leadership?"

Pay-Driven Employee

- "Do they ask about raises or incentives?"
- "Do they measure work in financial return?"
- "Do they negotiate effort vs reward?"

Position-Driven Employee

- "Do they ask about advancement?"
- "Do they seek leadership responsibility?"
- "Do they want decision-making authority?"

Figure 3. The Leadership Diagnostic Model

DOMINANT "P"	LEADERSHIP DIAGNOSTIC QUESTIONS
PRAISE (Recognition)	• Do they respond strongly to recognition? • Does appreciation increase performance?
PAY (Compensation)	• Do they ask about raises or incentives? • Do they measure work in financial return?
POSITION (Growth)	• Do they ask about effort vs. reward? • Do they ask about advancement? • Do they seek leadership responsibility?

Behavioral Indicators

Praise Drivers

- Responds strongly to recognition
- Appreciates feedback
- Values appreciation and respect

Leadership Tool: Recognition → Reinforcement → Performance

- *Pay Drivers*
- Focused on financial reward
- Negotiates workload for compensation
- Measures contribution vs reward

Leadership Tool: Performance → Value → Compensation

Position Drivers

- Wants responsibility and influence
- Interested in leadership roles
- Focused on career advancement

Leadership Tool: Development → Opportunity → Promotion

The Misread Complaint

The marketing manager repeatedly expressed frustration during team meetings. Her comments focused on: "No one notices the work we do." "Our contributions aren't visible." "Leadership doesn't understand the effort involved."

Her manager assumed she was seeking a promotion and began assigning her high-level projects. Her frustration grew. Eventually, in a one-on-one, she clarified, "I don't need a new title. I need our work acknowledged."

She was praise driven. The leader's assumption was that the driver was position. Wrong assumptions increase tension. What she needed was recognition—visible acknowledgment that her contributions mattered and that her effort was seen. What she received instead was a response rooted in advancement, a motivator that did not match her internal drive. That mismatch created friction, not fulfillment. When a leader uses the wrong motivator, even with good intentions, the employee feels misunderstood, the relationship strains, and engagement erodes in subtle but significant ways.

Pillar: Praise

When praise driven needs are misread as ambition for position, leaders increase responsibility while recognition remains absent, and frustration intensifies.

The Diagnostic Conversation Model

Instead of reacting, ask structured questions:

1. What part of your work energizes you most?
2. When do you feel most professionally satisfied?
3. What does success look like to you over next two years?
4. What frustrates you most about your current role?

Listen carefully:

- A praise driven response sounds like: "When my work is recognized."
- A pay driven response sounds like: "When I see financial progress."

- A position driven response sounds like: "When I'm trusted with more responsibility."

The language reveals the driver.

Scenario: Three Employees, Three Drivers

You manage three high performers.

In *t*his scenario, a manager oversees three high performing employees whose behaviors reveal three distinct motivational drivers. Employee A frequently asks, "How did I do?" This employee is praise driven; their repeated request for feedback signals a need for recognition, affirmation, and visible acknowledgment of their contributions.

Employee B wants to know bonus structures and commission ceilings. This employee is pay -driven; their focus on compensation mechanics shows that financial growth, earning potential, and clear reward pathways sustain their engagement.

Employee C asks about leadership meetings and exposure to strategic planning. This employee is position-driven; their questions reflect a desire for influence, visibility, and proximity to decision making as part of their advancement trajectory.

Together, these three employees demonstrate that motivation is not uniform, even among high performers. Each requires a different leadership approach, reinforcement strategy, and development pathway because the driver of their performance is not the same. Treating them identically costs you at least one. Precision replaces one size fits all.

The Leadership Risk of Assumption

Leaders often assume that high achievers are position driven; that young employees are pay-driven; and that quiet employees are self-motivated. None of these assumptions is reliable. Some quiet employees are praise-driven yet introverted. Some senior leaders remain deeply pay-driven. Some early-career employees prioritize growth over money. Diagnosis must be tailored to each individual. When leaders rely on assumptions instead of insight, they misread motivation, misapply incentives, and unintentionally create disengagement. The real leadership risk is not misunderstanding people, it is assuming you already understand them.

Department-Level Misalignment

A healthcare administrator managed a team of 25 people. After reviewing exit data, a pattern emerged: clinical staff left citing burnout, and administrative staff left citing stagnation. Two distinct drivers were at play. Clinical staff were praise-driven, they wanted acknowledgment for emotionally demanding work. Administrative staff were position-driven, they wanted advancement.

The administrator had applied pay adjustments across the board, yet turnover continued. After redesigning recognition systems for clinical teams and mapping development tracks for administrative staff, retention stabilized. Diagnosis changed strategy.

This demonstrates that retention improves only when leaders align the strategy to the motivator. The administrator's initial approach, universal pay adjustments, treated everyone as if the same need drove them. But once the true drivers were identified, the strategy shifted: praise-driven clinical staff received meaningful recognition, and position-driven administrative staff received clear development pathways. The result was stability. Diagnosis changed strategy, and strategy changed outcomes.

Pillar: Position

When leaders apply a single solution to multiple motivational drivers, misalignment persists. Retention stabilizes only when strategy aligns with what drives behavior. Retention improves only when leaders match the strategy to the motivator.

The Driver Shift Across Career Stages

Motivational drivers often evolve over a career, but not predictably or uniformly. Early in a career, praise and position often dominate. Individuals seek affirmation that their work matters and visibility into where their effort can lead. Recognition builds confidence, and opportunity signals possibility. As careers progress, pay and position often begin to balance. Financial growth becomes more significant, while advancement remains a measure of progress and credibility. Later in a career, pay and stability may become more important as priorities shift toward security, consistency, and long-term value exchange.

Evolution is not guaranteed. A person's career stage doesn't determine motivation, and age is not a reliable indicator of what drives behavior. Some early-career professionals are primarily pay-driven. Some senior leaders remain deeply praise-driven. Making assumptions is the fastest way to misalignment. Leaders who rely on demographic shortcuts instead of proper diagnosis use the wrong strategy confidently and quietly lose effectiveness.

The mandate is simple: do not assume. Observe. Pay attention to what individuals respond to, what they repeat, what frustrates them, and what they protect. Motivation shows in behavior long before it is openly expressed. Leaders who pay attention adjust accurately. Leaders who generalize misapply. In a system built on alignment, observation is not optional; it is foundational.

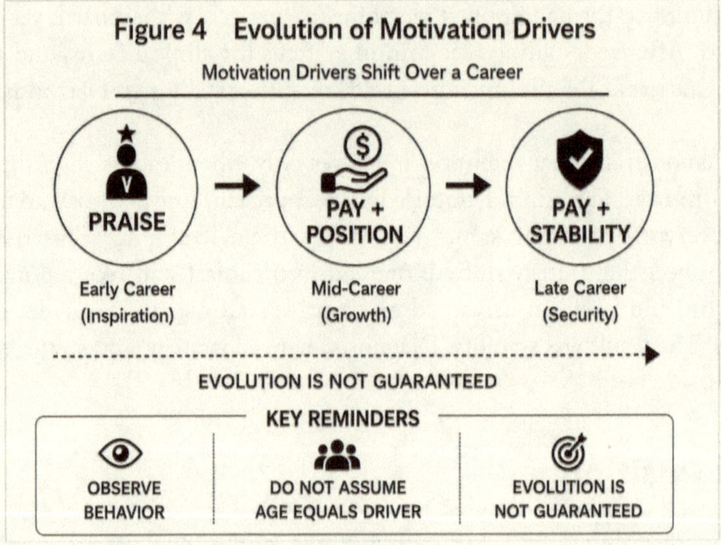

Figure 4 Evolution of Motivation Drivers

The Diagnostic Model

Use this three-step process:

1. *Step 1:* Observe Patterns – Track recurring language and behavior.

2. *Step 2:* Validate in Conversation – Ask structured growth questions.

3. *Step 3:* Apply a Micro Test – Adjust one driver and observe the response. When recognition increases and engagement rises, praise is likely dominant. When you define a growth pathway, and commitment deepens, position may be primary. When compensation alignment improves focus, Pay may be central. Diagnosis is iterative.

Iterative Diagnosis in Leadership

Effective leaders recognize that diagnosing motivational drivers is not a one-time event. Instead, it requires ongoing observation, conversation, and testing. By continuously monitoring behavioral and language patterns, validating assumptions through structured dialogue, and applying micro-tests, leaders refine their understanding of what motivates individuals. This iterative approach keep strategies remain aligned with evolving motivations, strengthening both engagement and organizational effectiveness.

The Organizational Diagnostic

At the department level, leaders can ask whether turnover is highest among high performers, whether raise requests are frequent, whether advancement questions are common, and whether feedback is often requested. These patterns reveal cultural misalignment, and indicate dominant drivers. Startups often lean toward position-driven, sales teams toward pay-driven, and service industries toward praise-driven. Context matters. The summary is simple: once a leader identifies a department's dominant driver, strategy becomes targeted rather than generic. Recognition systems can be shaped for praise-driven environments, compensation structures can be calibrated for pay-driven teams, and development pathways can be expanded for position-driven groups. Alignment begins with diagnosis, and diagnosis begins with patterns.

Leadership Dialogue Example

The manager said, "I've noticed you've been asking about next steps in your career. Tell me what growth looks like to you." The employee replied, "I want to lead a team eventually." The manager then said, "Let's define readiness milestones and timeline expectations."

This conversation stabilizes position-driven individuals.

The Cost of Getting It Wrong

When leaders misidentify, praise driven employees feel invisible, pay driven employees feel undervalued, and position driven employees feel stagnant. In every case, disengagement accelerates, retention declines, performance weakens, and trust erodes. Diagnosis is not optional, it is foundational.

The first cost is cultural. When leaders respond with the wrong driver, they unintentionally teach the organization that signals will be misunderstood. Employees stop sharing useful information. They become more cautious with feedback, less direct in conversations, and more likely to disengage silently than speak up early.

The second cost is operational. Misdiagnosis creates costly activity that doesn't change outcomes: raises that buy time but not commitment, added responsibilities that feel like a burden rather than growth, and recognition that feels generic instead of reinforcing. Meanwhile, the real issue remains untouched and performance begins to wobble because the employee no longer trusts the system to respond accurately.

This is why the language and behaviors in Table 1 should be treated as early warning indicators. If a leader can quickly translate a signal into the correct driver, correction stays simple. If they ignore the signal or respond with the wrong driver, the cost multiplies through turnover, re-hiring, slowed execution, and the quiet loss of discretionary effort that never appears on a report.

Diagnostic Leadership Summary

Consequence and Credibility

Misdiagnosis carries leadership consequences: failing to identify the true motivator not only delays progress but also compounds risk. When a leader applies the wrong driver, they unintentionally deepen disengagement, accelerate frustration, and normalize turnover as an expected outcome rather than a preventable one. Misdiagnosis creates a leadership blind spot. The leader believes they have addressed the issue, while the employee feels increasingly unseen. Over time, this gap leads to cultural erosion. The longer a leader waits to diagnose, the more costly the correction becomes financially, operationally, and culturally.

Diagnostic leadership strengthens credibility by demonstrating that decisions are grounded in understanding rather than assumption. When leaders take the time to identify what truly drives their people, employees experience leadership as intentional, not impulsive. They feel seen, not generalized.

This accuracy builds trust, and trust becomes the foundation for influence. A leader who diagnoses well earns the right to coach, to challenge, and to develop because employees believe the leader is acting with clarity, not convenience. Credibility grows when leadership decisions consistently align with what people need, not what leaders assume they need.

Reflection Audit – Chapter 3

1. List your top five performers.

2. Next to each name, write: Primary driver evidence supporting It risk if misaligned

3. If you cannot clearly articulate the evidence, you have not diagnosed deeply enough.

Leadership Shift

Leadership isn't about motivating people; it's about aligning strategy with what truly motivates them. The Three P's of People Development are not tactics to be applied reactively but insight drivers that must be identified before action. When leaders skip the identification step, they rely on assumptions that produce misalignment, such as misapplied praise, misdirected compensation, and stalled development. The result is predictable: effort declines, trust erodes, and retention weakens quietly.

Credible leadership is diagnostic. It observes before acting, interprets behavior before intervening, and applies strategy with precision rather than generosity. When leaders understand what drives behavior, their decisions stop signaling randomness and start reinforcing standards. Alignment replaces guesswork. Strategy gains traction. Leadership credibility grows, but because they respond correctly, not because leaders do more.

Lasting influence comes from diagnosing first, then acting.

Clarity isn't insight; it's a repeatable practice.

Chapter 1 revealed the illusion.

Chapter 2 revealed the erosion.

Chapter 3 built the diagnostic system.

Chapter 4 turns praise into reinforcement.

PART II - PRAISE

RECOGNITION AS A PERFORMANCE MULTIPLIER

Chapter 4

Recognition Is Not Kindness - It is Reinforcement

The Most Misunderstood Leadership Tool

Praise is often dismissed as soft, yet it can play a crucial role in motivating people. Leaders view it as encouragement, positivity, and a morale booster. However, when structured properly, praise isn't emotional; it's a way to reinforce behavior. What gets reinforced gets repeated. If you understand this principle, praise can become one of the most powerful tools a leader has for improving performance.

Most leaders treat praise as a personality trait, something you either naturally do or do not do. That framing is why praise remains inconsistent. In this model, praise is not a trait. It is a tool. It is the most accessible way for leaders to shape attention, define priorities, and make standards visible without changing headcount, budgets, or structure.

Encouragement is emotional support. Reinforcement is behavioral direction. Encouragement says, "Keep going." Reinforcement says, "Do that again." The second form is what cultures run on. People do not repeat what leaders admire in private; they repeat what leaders acknowledge in public and tie to results.

Most leaders default to encouragement because it feels relational and safe. It requires no standards, measurement, nor accountability. It comforts the person, but it does not clarify the work. Over time, a culture built primarily on encouragement becomes dependent on mood and motivation rather than discipline and direction.

Reinforcement is different. It names the behavior, ties it to a measurable outcome, and signals the standard the organization upholds. It reduces guesswork for everyone watching. When leaders consistently reinforce what "right" looks like- quality, speed, safety, margin, or service-employees stop chasing approval and start repeating performance.

When praise is tied to a defined standard – quality, speed, safety, margin, or service – it becomes a leadership signal. It tells the team what excellence looks like here. When praise is vague, delayed, and used to manage emotions, it stops reinforcing performance and creates confusion. The next section explains why reinforcement works so predictably and why leaders should treat it as a system, not a moment.

The Science Behind Reinforcement

Human behavior follows a predictable pattern:

- Actions
- Outcomes
- Reinforcement
- Repetition

Human behavior follows a predictable cycle: actions lead to outcomes, outcomes reinforce those actions, and reinforcement encourages repetition. This cycle operates within organizations, whether leaders intentionally create it or not. When a behavior results in recognition directly tied to performance standards, the brain perceives it as valuable. Over time, this perception shapes habits, effort, and beliefs about what matters.

For praise-driven individuals, this is especially impactful. Recognition isn't just a preference; it signals that their contribution matters. When high performance is reinforced, they lean in. Ignored behavior isn't neutral; it is viewed as nonessential. Effort that goes unacknowledged is quietly deprioritized, even when results appear strong.

This is where retention risk arises. Praise-driven individuals rarely protest or seek attention. Instead, they internalize invisibility. Work continues, but commitment declines. Over time, disengagement occurs not because performance has fallen, but because it was never reinforced. Culture shifts accordingly. What is recognized gets repeated. What is ignored gradually fades. When reinforcement disappears long enough, high performers don't burn out loudly; they leave quietly.

That is why reinforcement is not a form of soft leadership behavior; it is a structural retention mechanism. When leaders consistently reinforce the right behaviors, praise-driven individuals stay engaged, standards remain high, and culture stabilizes. When they do not, performance may persist temporarily, but loyalty does not.

When this cycle is broken, the first loss is not output but visibility. The most dangerous losses occur when top performers remain productive yet become psychologically unseen.

The Invisible Top Performer

A plant manager consistently exceeded production targets. Defect rates were the lowest at the facility, and turnover on his shift was minimal. Yet he rarely received acknowledgment.

The plant manager's reasoning was straightforward: "He's doing fine. He doesn't need praise." Within eight months, he accepted an offer elsewhere. During the exit interview, he said: "I just didn't feel like my work mattered here."

Performance that isn't reinforced tends to fade, especially among praise-driven individuals who internalize invisibility and may not seek attention. Recognize these traits by observing their reactions to acknowledgment and their engagement levels, which helps leaders tailor recognition strategies effectively.

Praise – Driven Employees

Praise-driven individuals thrive on specific acknowledgment and performance feedback. They internalize recognition deeply and equate acknowledgment with value and as confirmation that their work matters and is seen. For them, praise is not a bonus; it is a core motivational driver that reinforces purpose, direction, and identity within the organization.

When recognition is clear, timely, and tied to meaningful outcomes, employees accelerate. They become more engaged, more precise in their execution, and more aligned with expectations because they understand exactly what success looks like. Consistent praise builds confidence, which translates into sustained performance and discretionary effort.

However, when praise is absent, the shift is subtle yet significant. Praise-driven employees do not typically become disruptive or visibly disengaged. Instead, they withdraw quietly. Output may remain steady for a period of time, but energy, creativity, and initiative begin to decline. They stop going beyond what is required and start operating within the role's minimum boundaries.

This quiet disengagement is often misinterpreted as stability. Leaders may assume the employee is consistent, self-sufficient, or simply "not needing much." In reality, the employee is recalibrating their effort in the absence of reinforcement. Without recognition, they begin to question whether their contributions are valued or even noticed.

Over time, this lack of acknowledgment erodes connection. The employee may not voice dissatisfaction, but internally, they begin to detach from the organization's mission and from leadership. Eventually, they become more receptive to external opportunities—not necessarily for compensation, but because another environment may offer the visibility and validation they are missing.

Effective leaders recognize that praise must be intentional, not incidental. It must be:

1. Specific to the action or outcome

2. Timely to reinforce behavior in the moment

3. Connected to measurable or observable results

4. Aligned with defined performance standards

When delivered consistently, praise does more than motivate, it stabilizes performance, strengthens culture, and signals to employees that excellence is both recognized and expected.

The Difference Between Generic and Specific Praise

Generic praise sounds like, "Good job." Specific praise sounds like, "You reduced customer churn by 12% by restructuring the onboarding flow. That directly strengthened our retention standard."

The first feels good, while the second reinforces a standard. Specific praise connects behavior to organizational results; it teaches. Generic praise flatters, but specific praise multiplies.

Pillar: Praise

When Praise-driven performance is left unacknowledged, leaders misread silence as satisfaction recognizing disengagement after the loss has occurred.

Scenario: The Team Meeting

You are reviewing quarterly results.

Option A: "Everyone did great this quarter."

Option B: "Sarah's client recovery strategy prevented a $240,000 loss. That's the level of proactive leadership we expect."

Option B creates cultural clarity. Public and specific praise defines standards.

The Recognition Multiplier Model

Effective praise must meet four criteria:

1. Specific
2. Timely
3. Linked to measurable outcomes
4. Reinforcing a defined standard

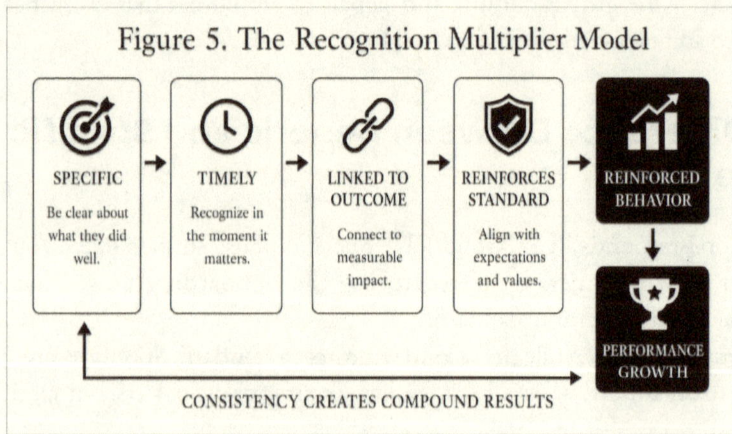

Remove any one of these, and the impact decreases.

Culture Shift Through Recognition

A hospitality executive implemented a structured recognition program. Every weekly meeting included one performance-based recognition, one value-based recognition, and one innovation-based recognition. No compensation changes were made. Within six months, employee engagement scores increased, guest satisfaction improved, and voluntary turnover declined. Nothing financially changed. What changed was reinforcement. Recognition reshaped behavior.

Pillar: Praise

When recognition is clear, consistent, and aligned with performance, values, and innovation, behavior changes without affecting pay. Praise reinforces what the organization wants repeated and, when used intentionally, reshapes culture, boosts engagement, and reduces turnover.

When Praise Backfires

Praise becomes harmful when it is excessive, rewards mediocrity, is disconnected from performance, or distributed for political reasons. When everyone is praised equally, standards become unclear. Praise must be earned, not handed out freely.

Dialogue Example: Specific Reinforcement

The manager said, "I want to highlight your response to the system outage. You stayed calm, coordinated cross-functional support, and restored operations within 90 minutes. That's leadership under pressure." The employee replied, "I appreciate that."

What was reinforced? Calm, coordination, speed, and ownership. The next crisis will follow the same pattern.

The Hidden Harm of Not Giving Recognition

Some leaders believe withholding praise makes people tougher, but it actually causes doubt. Without positive feedback, high performers tend to interpret silence negatively. They quietly but urgently ask: "Does my work matter here?"

When that question goes unanswered, disengagement begin not out of defiance or decline, but as withdrawal. Effort becomes more careful. Initiative decreases. Discretionary energy diminishes. Leaders who show and encourage recognition practices can help team members feel safe and trusted, boosting their confidence and commitment.

Diagnostic Questions for Leaders

1. When was the last time you publicly linked praise to measurable outcomes?

2. Do you use performance-based recognition models?

3. Does praise align with standards or personal traits?

4. Who on your team openly reacts to recognition?

If you can't give a clear answer, praise is unintentional — not deliberate.
List three individuals who may be praise-driven.
For each, answer:

- How often do I recognize their measurable outcomes?
- Is recognition tied to standards?
- Have I unintentionally allowed invisibility?

Recognition is not a bonus; it is reinforcement. Include specific metrics or KPIs to assess whether your recognition system enhances engagement, performance, and culture, ensuring your efforts are strategic and impactful.

Reflection Audit – Chapter 4

1. In the last two weeks, have you reinforced a specific behavior—or just complimented effort?
2. Is your recognition tied to a defined standard (quality, speed, safety, margin, service), or to personality traits?
3. Are you recognizing outcomes that are measurable, or are you rewarding visibility, likeability, and noise?
4. Which top performer has been consistently delivering results with little to no reinforcement?
5. Where might praise inflation be weakening your standards (recognizing everyone equally, rewarding mediocrity, or praising without proof)?

If reinforcement is vague or inconsistent, standards drift—and praise-driven talent quietly detaches.

Leadership Shift

Praise is not about ego; it is about clarity. When leaders use praise intentionally, they clarify expectations, help team members feel appreciated, and inspire continued effort.

Ignoring this can create doubt, causing employees to question whether their work truly matters, which lowers motivation.

This is why praise forms the foundation of the Three P's of People Development Model. Before pay reflects value, and before position upholds ambition, reinforcement must set direction. Praise shows people what success looks like here. It signals what the organization protects, rewards, and expects. Without that signal, even the strongest systems weaken. Performance may persist for a while, but alignment does not.

Reinforcement is essential to leadership; it forms its foundation. Without it, standards become unclear, motivation erodes, and retention is unpredictable. With reinforcement, performance stabilizes, loyalty grows, and culture becomes deliberate rather than accidental. Without reinforcement, no system endures.

When performance isn't reinforced, it fades and top performers leave.

Recognition that isn't structured becomes noise.

Chapter 4 made praise a performance tool.

Chapter 5 makes it scalable.

Chapter 5

Designing a Scalable Recognition System

Individual Praise Is Not Enough

Many leaders believe they are effective at recognition because they personally give praise. They point to moments when they acknowledged strong performance, thanked an employee, or highlighted a win. While these moments matter, they are often mistaken for a system. Culture, however, is not built on moments, it is built on consistency.

Recognition that depends solely on a leader's memory, mood, or availability is inherently unstable. If praise happens only when you remember, it is inconsistent. If it is inconsistent, it is unreliable. If it is unreliable, it does not shape behavior. Employees cannot align with a standard they do not see consistently reinforced.

In these environments, recognition becomes selective rather than systematic. Some employees receive acknowledgment because they are visible, vocal, or closely connected to leadership, while others, often high performers go unnoticed. Over time, this creates perception gaps. Recognition begins to feel subjective, and when it does, trust erodes.

Even well-intentioned leaders cannot sustain recognition at scale. As teams grow, complexity increases. Priorities shift, time compresses, and what was once manageable becomes inconsistent. Without structure, recognition becomes reactive rather than intentional, triggered by standout moments rather than embedded in daily operations.

Effective organizations understand that recognition must move beyond personality and into process. It must be designed, not improvised. Recognition should be triggered by defined standards, reinforced through consistent behaviors, and distributed across all levels of the organization not centralized in one leader.

This is where many leadership efforts fall short. Leaders attempt to solve engagement challenges through personal effort rather than through organizational design. They work harder to recognize rather than build systems that ensure recognition happens regardless of who is leading, who is present, or how busy the environment becomes.

When recognition is system-driven, it becomes predictable. When it is predictable, it becomes credible. And when it is credible, it begins to shape behavior at scale.

Individual praise still matters, but it is not enough. Without a structured approach, even the best leaders will fall short of building a culture where recognition consistently drives performance, engagement, and retention.

The Difference Between Moments and Systems

Leaders confuse recognition with culture because moments feel meaningful. But culture is not built by isolated wins. It is built when reinforcement is repeatable, standard-based, and consistent across teams.

A moment is when you offer congratulations to someone after a big win, while a system is when your organization has a structured reinforcement process linked to measurable standards.

Moments inspire, but systems multiply. A repeatable reinforcement rhythm turns recognition into a cultural standard instead of a random event.

The Founder Who Struggled to Scale Culture

A growing tech company was known for its strong internal culture. In its early years, the founder personally recognized high performers weekly. As the company grew beyond 150 employees, recognition decreased. The founder was stretched thin, meetings increased, and growth accelerated.

Within a year, engagement scores declined. High performers felt unseen. Internal promotions decreased. The founder realized something critical: culture was tied to his personality — not a system. When recognition depends on one person, culture suffers when that person becomes overwhelmed.

He implemented standardized team-level recognition rituals, performance-aligned recognition criteria, and leadership accountability for reinforcement. Engagement recovered, and culture scaled.

Pillar: Praise

When praise exists as a personality trait rather than a system, culture scales only until the individual at its center becomes unavailable.

An effective recognition system operates on three levels:

1. Organizational Level: Publicly reinforce company-wide standards.

2. Department Level: Recognition based on specific performance metrics linked to tangible results.

3. Individual Level: Customized reinforcement aligned with individual drivers.

Figure 5.1

The Recognition Architecture Model

An effective recognition system operates on three levels:

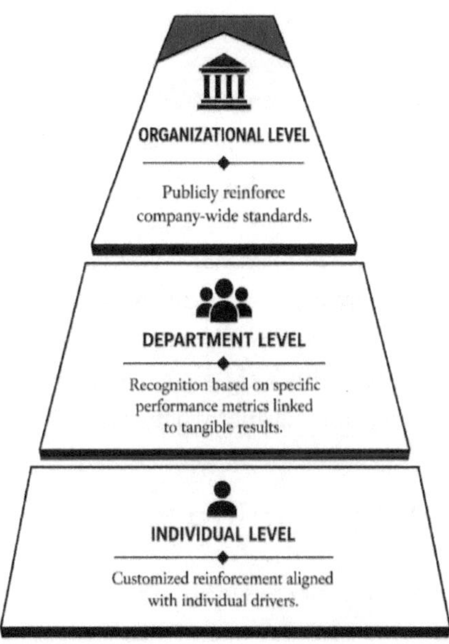

When all three operate consistently, recognition becomes predictable and powerful.

Organizational-Level Reinforcement

At the highest level, praise shapes identity.

Questions to answer:

- What behaviors reflect our standards?
- What performance metrics define excellence?
- What actions merit public visibility?

Recognition at this level should:

- Reinforce company values
- Emphasize measurable outcomes
- Model decision-making standards

Example of visible standards:

Don't say, "Congratulations to the sales team." Instead, say, "The sales team exceeded quarterly revenue by 18% while reducing discount rates. That reinforces our discipline standard."

Department-Level Recognition

Department leaders must translate company standards into operational behaviors. For example, customer service focuses on response time, resolution accuracy, and client satisfaction, while operations focus on efficiency metrics, error reduction, and process optimization.

Each department should have defined reinforcement triggers, weekly recognition moments, and measurable performance indicators. Recognition without metrics becomes political, driven by perception rather than actual performance. Recognition with metrics becomes credible because it ties acknowledgment to measurable standards, removes ambiguity, and clarifies what success looks like.

Individual-Level Recognition

At the individual level, accuracy matters most. The goal is not to recognize everyone the same way; it is to reinforce what each person is optimizing for."

- Praise-driven: responds to frequent, specific reinforcement tied to standards.
- Pay-driven: values recognition that connects contribution to measurable financial impact.
- Position-driven: responds strongly when recognition affirms readiness,

leadership capacity, and expanded responsibility.

The system must remain flexible enough to personalize reinforcement without weakening standards.

Scenario: Recognition Breakdown

A regional manager starts monthly awards. Every department nominates someone. The same people rotate through the awards. Within months, recognition loses its meaning.

Why? It became ceremonial. Ceremonial recognition rewards presence. Strategic recognition rewards performance.

Building the Weekly Reinforcement Rhythm

To scale praise, build a structured cadence:

- *Weekly*: One recognition based on performance per team.
- *Monthly:* One innovation recognition award.
- *Quarterly:* One culture-defining recognition linked to measurable impact

Consistency creates expectations, and these expectations shape culture.

The 15-Minute Ritual

A logistics company implemented a simple weekly ritual. The first 15 minutes of every Monday meeting were dedicated to reviewing one measurable win, publicly linking it to standards, and acknowledging the individuals responsible. The ritual required no budget.

After 90 days, team initiative grew. Peer recognition developed naturally. Performance discussions improved. Recognition shifted from being manager-driven to culture-driven.

Pillar: Praise

When praise becomes a consistent system rather than a random act, recognition extends beyond the leader and shapes the culture.

The Leadership Cascade Effect

If senior leaders do not model structured recognition, middle managers will not prioritize it.

Recognition must cascade:

- Executive Level
- Regional Level
- Department Level
- Team Level

When reinforcement flows top-down, it stabilizes standards organization-wide.

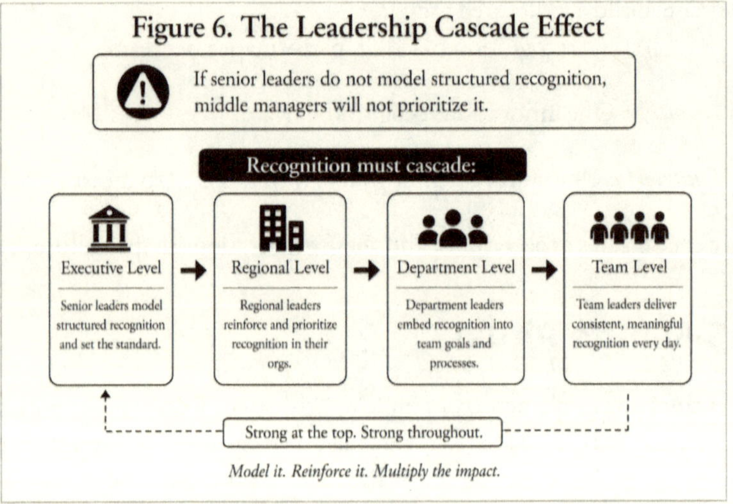

Avoiding Recognition Inflation

Over-recognition dilutes standards. When everything is praised, nothing is distinguished. High performers notice when mediocre performance is celebrated. That weakens trust.

- Defined standards
- Measurable outcomes

- Clear behavioral examples

Reflection Audit – Chapter 5

1. Is recognition currently driven by personality or system?
2. Do department leaders have structured reinforcement moments?
3. Are recognition criteria documented?
4. Does praise reinforce standards or popularity?

If recognition is inconsistent, the culture becomes unstable.

Leadership Shift

Without systematized praise, excellence goes unseen. With it, excellence becomes repeatable. High performance may persist for a while, but without reinforcement, it loses importance, purpose, and momentum. Over time, what is not visibly reinforced is quietly deprioritized, and the culture shifts accordingly. When structured and intentional, praise prevents that decline by anchoring standards, sustaining engagement, and making excellence repeatable.

The leadership shift is moving from personal recognition to organizational reinforcement. Individual leaders can create moments, but only systems ensure consistency. A scalable recognition system defines what gets reinforced, when it gets reinforced, and who is accountable for reinforcing it. That structure protects standards when leaders are busy, teams are stretched, and priorities compete.

When Praise becomes a system, it stabilizes behavior and strengthens culture. But it remains only one pillar. As performance grows, praise must eventually connect to Pay and Position to remain credible. The next chapter defines when recognition stops being enough—and why disciplined leaders know when to shift from reinforcement to progression.

Praise is structural, metrics give it credibility, and culture carries it forward.

Chapter 6

When Praise Is Not Enough - The Limits of Recognition

The Recognition Ceiling

There comes a moment in every high performer's career when praise no longer satisfies. Early in development, recognition fuels confidence. Midway through growth, recognition fuels momentum. But eventually, recognition without advancement or compensation feels hollow. Leaders who over-rely on praise hears: "I appreciate the acknowledgment, but what's next?" That question signals a driver shift.

The recognition ceiling is not a failure of appreciation; it is a signal of progression. Praise can reinforce standards and sustain early commitment, but it cannot substitute for a visible future or a fair value exchange. When a high performer keeps hearing reinforcement without seeing movement, the unintended message is: "We see your output, but nothing changes because of it."

Leaders misread this stage because performance often remains high. The employee is still dependable. Deadlines are still met. Results still show up on the report. But internally, the primary driver has shifted. Praise no longer answers the question the employee is now asking: "What does this lead to?" or "Does the exchange still make sense?" When those questions go unanswered, commitment becomes conditional.

The correct response is not to praise louder. It is to diagnose the new primary driver and adjust the system around it. For some, that means clarifying the pay contract and what measurable increase justifies the next tier. For others, it means clarifying the position and what readiness milestones define advancement and what experiences must be earned first. Praise should remain, but now it must connect to structure: reinforcement that points toward compensation alignment or a visible pathway.

The Loyal High Performer

A senior operations analyst consistently delivered measurable results. Her director regularly praised her work in meetings and recognized her contributions during executive reviews. Engagement appeared strong.

One afternoon, she requested a private chat. "I value the recognition," she said. "But I need to understand how this translates into growth."

The director realized something important. Praise reinforced effort, but it did not address advancement or financial growth. She was no longer primarily driven by praise. Her motivation drive had shifted toward position and pay. Recognition had reached its limit.

Pillar: Praise

When praise is no longer tied to advancement or financial growth, high performers shift their motivational driver and recognition alone ceases to motivate.

The Three Signs Praise Has Reached Its Limit

1. *The "What's Next?" Question:* When employees ask about progression after consistent recognition, they signal evolution.

2. *Compensation Comparison:* When high performers begin referencing market value or peers' earnings, praise alone is no longer sufficient to motivate.

3. *The Responsibility Request:* When employees seek a broader scope, greater decision-making authority, or strategic involvement, advancement becomes a primary focus.

Ignoring these signals leads to stagnation.

The Praise Trap

Some leaders overuse praise because it feels safe. Recognition costs nothing. Raises require budgeting. Promotions require structural change. So leaders tend to choose the easiest option.

On the surface, this seems positive. Employees are acknowledged, and effort is recognized. The environment feels encouraging. But when praise becomes the default response to every performance gap, it loses its effectiveness. What was once meaningful becomes routine, and what was routine becomes expected.

The problem is not praise itself; it is imbalance.

When praise substitute for pay or position, it creates a disconnect between effort and outcome. Employees may hear they are doing exceptional work, but if that message is not reinforced with compensation or advancement, the signal becomes confusing. Over time, credibility erodes. Recognition without alignment breeds doubt: If I am performing at a high level, why is nothing changing?

This is where the praise trap takes hold. Leaders believe they are motivating, but they delay necessary decisions. Instead of addressing compensation gaps, they offer encouragement. Instead of creating advancement pathways, they offer appreciation. Instead of aligning performance with tangible outcomes, they reinforce effort with words alone.

Initially, employees may respond positively. Praise satisfies the need for acknowledgment. But as performance remains stagnant without corresponding progress, the impact shifts. What once felt motivating begins to feel like deflection. Employees start to interpret praise not as recognition but as a substitution for action.

High performers are sensitive to this imbalance. They do not expect immediate rewards, but they do expect alignment. When praise is not matched by pay or position over time, it signals that performance is recognized but not valued at the level it deserves.

Eventually, praise without progression breeds disengagement. Employees begin to reduce discretionary effort, not out of resistance but out of recalibration. They adjust their performance to match the return they receive. In some cases, they begin exploring environments where recognition is reinforced by tangible outcomes.

Effective leadership requires discipline across all three drivers. Praise should reinforce behavior. Pay should validate contribution. Position should signal future opportunity. When one is overused at the expense of the others, the system breaks down.

Praise is powerful, but only when it is aligned.

Scenario: The High-Achiever Plateau

You oversee a Team Lead who consistently surpasses expectations. Their performance is not sustained. They deliver results, stabilize operations, support peers, and often take on responsibilities beyond their defined role. They are reliable, respected, and increasingly influential within the team.

You recognize this. You publicly acknowledge their performance in meetings. You highlight their leadership qualities. You thank them often and hold them up as an example of excellence. From your perspective, you are doing what a leader should do, reinforcing strong performance and maintaining morale.

For a time, this works. The Team Lead continues to perform. They remain engaged, responsive, and committed. Their consistency creates the appearance of stability. There are no complaints, visible signs of dissatisfaction, or indication that anything is wrong.

Then, after a year, they begin exploring external opportunities.

This shift often feels unexpected. Leaders are caught off guard because, from their perspective, the employee was recognized, supported, and valued. The underlying issue was never about recognition alone.

Recognition reinforces performance, but it does not improve status or pay.

Over time, high achievers evaluate their environment by alignment, not by intention. They begin to assess whether their level of contribution is matched by tangible progression. Are they positioned for advancement? Is their compensation reflective of their impact? Is their role evolving to match the level at which they are already operating?

When the answers to these questions are consistently no, a plateau forms.

High Performers Plateau

This plateau is not immediately visible. Performance remains high, but growth stalls. The employee is producing at the next level without being placed there. They are contributing beyond their role without being compensated. They are demonstrating leadership without formal recognition as a leader in structure or status.

At this point, praise begins to lose its effectiveness.

What once felt motivating now feels repetitive. What once signaled appreciation now signals delay. The employee does not necessarily reject the praise, but they begin to reinterpret it. Rather than viewing it as recognition of value, they come to see it as a substitute for progress.

High performers do not expect immediate promotion or constant raises, but they do expect a trajectory. They look for signs that their current performance is leading somewhere and that there is a pathway from effort to outcome.

When that pathway is unclear or absent, they create one themselves.

Exploring external opportunities is not always driven by dissatisfaction. It is often driven by clarity. The belief that other organizations offer a visible link between performance and progression, clearer roles, defined advancement paths, and compensation structures that reflect contribution. What was missing internally becomes visible externally.

Consistent excellence should result in progression.

Effective leaders anticipate this moment before it happens. They do not wait for disengagement or departure signals. They actively align all three drivers:

- Praise to reinforce performance
- Pay to validate contribution
- Position to create forward movement

When these are aligned, high achievers accelerate within the organization. When they are not, high achievers plateau, and eventually leave. The loss is not sudden. It is structural.

The Retention Miscalculation

A regional retail manager had an outstanding store director. Quarterly results were excellent, and recognition was steady. However, pay structures hadn't been adjusted in three years. Competitors began offering slightly higher salaries. The store director accepted an offer with only a seven percent raise.

The regional manager was surprised. "But you were so appreciated here." Appreciation does not outweigh perceived undervaluation.

Pay-driven individuals require alignment between contribution and compensation. Praise cannot substitute for financial clarity.

Pillar: Pay

For pay-driven talent, sustained high performance without regular compensation alignment signals undervaluation; if pay doesn't reflect contribution, recognition alone won't keep them from leaving.

Motivational Drivers

Motivational drivers are not fixed. An employee might begin their career as praise-driven, with recognition boosting confidence and encouraging early effort.

As confidence and contributions grow, pay may become a key indicator, signaling that value and output are being fairly exchanged. Later in a career, position may become more important, as individuals pursue growth, authority, and a clear path forward.

Since drivers change, leaders must regularly reevaluate them. Assumptions fade over time. What once motivated performance won't always sustain it, and without intentional reevaluation, alignment gradually weakens.

Examples of Reassessing Drivers

Praise – Pay Shift

A high-performing analyst who once responded strongly to recognition begins to ask how performance ratings affect bonuses and salary progression. Praise still matters, but questions now center on equity, pay structure, and timing. The motivational driver has shifted from validation to value exchange.

Praise – Position Shift

An employee who previously sought visibility now requests developmental assignments, opportunities to engage with senior leaders, or involvement in strategic initiatives. Recognition is valued, but it's no longer enough. Their underlying need has shifted toward growth and career trajectory.

Pay – Position Shift

A consistently compensated top performer stops negotiating bonuses and instead asks about leadership opportunities, decision-making authority, or team ownership. Compensation is no longer the primary driver; advancement and influence are.

Position – Pay Shift

A leader who once focused on titles and scope begins to prioritize long-term financial benefits, equity participation, or compensation structure as responsibilities stabilize. The focus shifts from expansion to sustainability.

Consistent Performance, Evolving Language

An employee's output remains strong, but their language shifts from "Is this good work?" to "What does this lead to?"often signaling that a reassessment may be needed.

The Compensation Legitimacy Principle

Recognition fosters emotional loyalty by affirming that an individual's effort, contribution, and presence matter. Compensation builds structural loyalty by reinforcing that value in tangible, measurable ways. When compensation does not reflect contribution, trust diminishes because words and outcomes no longer align, external exploration increases as employees quietly test their market value, and praise feels inadequate, no matter how sincerely it is given. In those moments, recognition alone cannot offset misalignment. The leader must ensure pay progression reflects measurable value so that appreciation and reward move together, reinforcing commitment instead of eroding it.

Dialogue Example: The Pivot Moment

The employee said, "I appreciate the recognition I've received. But I want to talk about growth." The manager responded, "That's fair," and added, "Let's discuss both compensation alignment and advancement readiness."

The employee acknowledges the value of recognition is an indicator that their praise needs have been met; but their request signals a shift. They are no longer seeking recognition; they are seeking advancement. They are asking the leader to move beyond recognition and toward the primary driver that aligns with their motivation.

The manager's response recognizes the shift in motivation and adjusts accordingly. Instead of offering more encouragement or reassurance, the manager redirects the conversation toward the systems that govern growth: compensation alignment (Pay) and advancement readiness (Position).

This pivot matters. It demonstrates that development is not emotional; it is structural. Praise acknowledges contribution. Pay validates value. Position expands responsibility. When an employee signals readiness to move from one driver to another, the leader's role is to meet them at that level with clarity, criteria, and a pathway.

In this exchange, the manager does exactly that. They shift from reinforcing what the employee has done to outlining what the employee must demonstrate next. The conversation becomes less about feeling appreciated and more about readiness for advancement.

This pivot shifts the focus from emotional reinforcement to structural development. That transition signifies leadership maturity.

The Risk of Delayed Adjustment

If leaders wait until resignation is imminent to adjust compensation or advancement pathways, they have already lost leverage. Reactive pay adjustments send the message, "We only value you when you threaten to leave." Strategic pay alignment signals, "We recognize your value consistently." Timing matters.

Diagnostic Signal – Praise (Delayed Reinforcement)

If leaders wait until disengagement becomes visible before recognizing performance, they have already lost influence. Reactive praise signals, "Your effort is noticed only when it starts to fade." Strategic recognition signals, "Your contribution is consistently seen and reinforced."

Reflection Audit – Chapter 6

1. Who on your team has received repeated praise without structural progression?
2. Are pay structures aligned with measurable outcomes?
3. Do advancement conversations occur proactively or reactively?
4. Have any high performers recently referenced market value?

If the answer to #4 is yes, alignment may be slipping.

Leadership Shift

Praise establishes value through reinforcement. But at higher levels of performance, value must be legitimized through structure. Pay affirms contribution, and compensation reinforces that the exchange is fair. Without pay alignment, praise begins to feel symbolic. When praise and pay are aligned, retention stabilizes. When they are not, loyalty diminishes.

The leadership shift in this chapter is simple: stop using one driver to carry what requires two. Recognition is a performance multiplier, but it has a ceiling. When a high performer's language shifts from "Is this good?" to "What does this lead to?" the leader's job is to adjust the system, not to repeat the same reinforcement with greater volume and frequency.

Respond with discipline. Diagnose the driver, then make the next step measurable by clarifying what value increases compensation, and define what readiness earns expanded scope. Praise remains essential, but it must now point toward pay and position alignment. That is how reinforcement becomes progression and why the next section resets compensation as an exchange.

Praise establishes value. *Pay legitimizes value.*

PART III - PAY

COMPENSATION AS A VALUE EXCHANGE

Praise creates momentum; it doesn't replace progression.

Chapter 6 defined the limits of recognition.

Chapter 7 resets pay as an exchange.

Chapter 7

Compensation Is Not Generosity - It is an Exchange

The Emotional Mistake Leaders Make

Leaders often view compensation emotionally, focusing on loyalty, effort, tenure, and likeability. However, compensation is not a reward for simply being present; it is an exchange of measurable value. When compensation becomes emotional, the company culture starts to weaken. But when it becomes strategic, performance sees improvement.

The Value Exchange Principle

Compensation must always address one question: "What measurable value is being exchanged for this financial increase?" If this question cannot be clearly answered, entitlement begins to grow.

The value exchange principle is simple: **increased pay equals increased measurable output**. Without the second component, pay is a gift not a contract.

The Raise That Backfired

A mid-sized consulting firm raised salaries for all employees following a profitable year, aiming to demonstrate appreciation.

Within nine months, productivity leveled off as accountability discussions grew, yet revenue growth slowed. The root cause was that raises were not tied to performance standards, with no new metrics introduced or additional responsibilities assigned.

Compensation increased, expectations stayed the same, and entitlement quietly took the place of motivation.

Pillar: Pay

When pay increases without meeting performance expectations, compensation reinforces entitlement rather than contribution.

The Entitlement Cycle

When pay increases happen without clear, measurable outcomes:

1. Compensation rises.
2. Expectations remain unclear.
3. Performance stabilizes or declines.
4. Leaders hesitate to enforce accountability.
5. Culture weakens.

Breaking this cycle requires discipline.

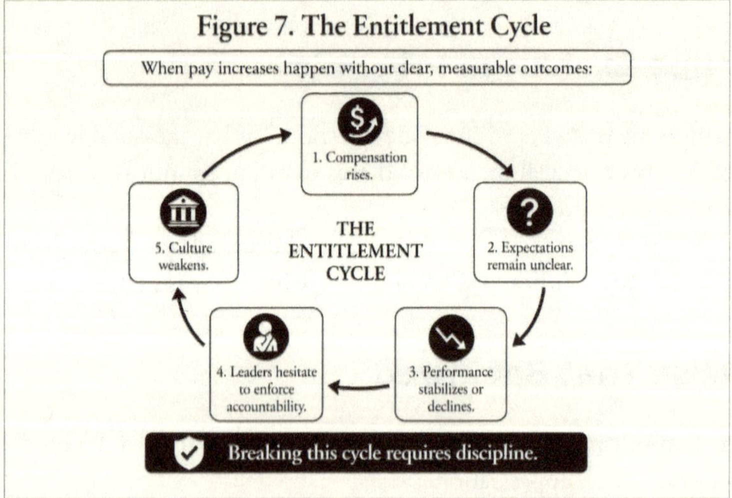

Compensation as Contract

Compensation is a professional agreement, not an emotional gesture. It sets clear terms and expectations, stating, "In exchange for this level of value, you will receive this level of pay." The agreement is based on contribution, results, and measurable impact; not intent, effort, or personal circumstances. When either side changes; the value delivered increases, decreases, or shifts in scope and renegotiation is necessary to restore alignment. Framing compensation this way brings clarity and fairness because the conversation focuses on outcomes rather than feelings. This approach removes emotion from pay discussions, allowing leaders and employees to engage in objective, respectful dialogue centered on value, growth, and accountability rather than justification or resentment.

Scenario: The Tenure Argument

In the tenure-based conversation, the employee said, "I've been here three years. I think it's time for a raise." A reactive manager responds, "You're right. You've been loyal." A strategic manager responds, "Let's define what additional measurable value justifies moving to the next compensation tier."

Tenure refers to the length of time an employee has spent with an organization. Compensation, on the other hand, is the value-the measurable contribution, impact, and results-that an employee delivers during that period. The two are not interchangeable; mixing them up causes instability because time alone does not ensure ongoing value. When pay is based on tenure instead of contribution, performance signals become unclear, accountability diminishes, and high performers may question the fairness of the system. Stability is achieved only when compensation consistently reflects worth, not just tenure. Confusing the two leads to instability.

That clarity requires leaders to define, track, and reward performance metrics that make value visible, measurable, and repeatable.

The Compensation Architecture Model

A strong pay system includes defined compensation levels, clear performance metrics for each level, documented readiness standards, review schedules, and transparent expectations. When employees know how to earn more, performance becomes intentional. When compensation feels random, resentment grows.

The Performance Ladder Reset

A manufacturing executive inherited a workforce with unclear pay structures. Raises were granted inconsistently over the years, with some employees receiving increases, while others saw no changes. This inconsistency created frustration among staff and made long-term financial planning difficult. Employees compared salaries, morale declined, and accountability became inconsistent.

To restore alignment, the executive established clear pay levels, measurable production targets for each level, and written documentation outlining expectations. Within twelve months, output increased, pay complaints decreased, and accountability improved. Clarity stabilized the culture.

The Psychology of Pay-Driven Employees

Pay-driven individuals track market benchmarks, compare earning potential, associate financial growth with achievement, and respond strongly to performance-based incentives. They are not greedy. They are performance-oriented.

Diagnostic Signal: When compensation progression is clear, they accelerate. When it is opaque, they disengage.

Dialogue Example: Structured Compensation Conversation

The manager said, “You’ve requested a raise. Let’s review your current output.” The employee replied, “I’ve exceeded my targets.” The manager responded, “You’ve met them. To move to the next tier, output must increase by 15%, and mentoring responsibilities must expand. Let’s define the timeline.”

Why this works:

- Removes emotion from the conversation
- Defines measurable criteria
- Creates clarity around expectations
- Aligns compensation with value

Result: Compensation becomes structured; not sentimental.

When Pay Is the Primary Driver

For pay-driven employees, compensation should be tied directly to measurable results, supported by transparent metrics, reinforced through quarterly review checkpoints, and never diluted by vague promises. Ambiguity weakens commitment. Clarity strengthens drive.

The Cost of Avoiding Pay Conversations

Leaders often delay compensation discussions out of fear of conflict. That avoidance creates assumptions, misinformation, market comparison, and distrust. Strategic pay conversations reduce anxiety. Silence increases it.

Reflection Audit – Chapter 7

1. Are compensation tiers clearly defined?
2. Are raises tied to measurable performance?
3. Have you documented readiness criteria for advancement?
4. Is compensation perceived as fair and transparent?

If the answer to any of these is unclear, alignment is at risk.

Leadership Shift

Compensation is not generosity; it is an exchange. When pay is treated emotionally, based on loyalty, tenure, or likability; the standards blur and accountability weakens. When pay is treated as a contract and is tied to measurable value; fairness becomes clear, performance becomes intentional, and trust stabilizes.

The leadership shift is one of discipline. Leaders must define compensation tiers, document the metrics that justify movement, and have proactive conversations that remove ambiguity before resentment forms. Pay questions are never just about money; they are about clarity. When the value exchange is undefined, entitlement grows. When it is defined, effort has a target and accountability has a foundation.

Praise builds momentum, but pay protects standards by demonstrating that performance is valued in tangible terms. When pay is aligned, Position becomes credible because advancement decisions are no longer forced to compensate for an unfair exchange. Chapter 8 shows what happens when pay systems drift—overpaying for underperformance, underpaying for excellence, and quietly rewriting the culture.

Praise builds culture. *Disciplined pay protects it.*

Pay must reinforce standards—or it quietly rewrites them.

Chapter 7 defined pay as a disciplined contract.

Chapter 8 exposes where pay systems break.

Chapter 8

Avoiding the Compensation Trap

Where Pay Systems Break Down

The Two Most Dangerous Errors

Compensation systems rarely collapse loudly. They erode quietly through two predictable mistakes: overpaying underperformers and underpaying high performers. Both destroy culture, but in different ways.

Error #1: Overpaying Underperformers

This usually happens gradually. An employee has been with the company for years. Raises were given gradually. Expectations were never adjusted. Over time, compensation exceeds contribution. The leader knows this but avoids addressing it.

Overpaying underperformers is one of the most corrosive compensation errors an organization can tolerate. Unlike isolated performance issues, this mistake rarely appears as a single failure. It accumulates slowly, quietly reshaping standards, weakening accountability, and distorting how value is measured across culture.

This error typically develops incrementally. An employee gains tenure. Raises are granted consistently. Expectations are never recalibrated. Over time, compensation continues to rise while contributions stabilize or decline. The gap between pay and performance widens gradually, and leadership grows accustomed to it. Eventually, compensation no longer reflects current value; it reflects history.

Leaders are usually aware of the imbalance. What prevents correction is not ignorance but avoidance. Addressing overpayment requires difficult conversations: redefining responsibilities, strengthening performance expectations, revisiting role fit, or confronting whether the individual should remain in the position. These actions feel disruptive, so silence seems easier. That silence is costly.

The Untouchable Veteran

A distribution company had a warehouse supervisor with 18 years of tenure. Compensation had grown steadily over time. However, efficiency had declined, team morale had weakened, and standards had become inconsistent.

The executive team acknowledged the problem privately, but no one addressed it publicly. High performers noticed.

Within a year, two rising managers left, productivity declined, and informal resentment spread. Overpaying one person costs the organization three others. Compensation decisions are closely watched.

Overpaid underperformers are rarely labeled as such. More often, they are described as "reliable," "experienced," or "part of the fabric of the organization." Their historical value overshadows their current contribution, and compensation becomes insulated from scrutiny.

What leadership often overlooks is that compensation is not judged in isolation. It is evaluated relation to others.

High performers notice when accountability is uneven. They observe when tenure protects compensation more than results do. They see who is allowed to coast—and who is expected to make up for the drift.

The presence of an overpaid underperformer does not foster loyalty. It signals tolerance.

Pillar: Pay

Compensation should match current contribution, not just tenure; when overpaying for underperformance, high performers become disengaged and leave, and the culture bears the cost.

The Cultural Signal of Overpayment

When underperformers are compensated at levels disproportionate to their contribution, the organization sends an unmistakable message: performance standards are negotiable.

Accountability weakens because consequences are unclear. Standards blur because output and reward are disconnected. Trust erodes because effort feels misdirected.

High performers begin to question whether sustained excellence is worth the effort when compensation seems disconnected from results. Over time, discretionary effort fades, not through rebellion, but through resignation.

Overpaying one underperformer affects more than one role. It subtly rewrites the rules for everyone watching.

Pay communicates what leadership values, and misaligned pay signals confusion.

Why Leaders Delay Correction

Leaders often rationalize overpayment by focusing on past service, personal relationships, or the fear of destabilization. They assume that correcting compensation issues will cause disruption.

What they miss is that misalignment already *is* disruption—just delayed and decentralized.

While leaders postpone the conversation, culture absorbs the cost.

Compensation should reflect current contribution, not historical presence. When pay is disconnected from performance, compensation becomes entitlement rather than exchange. Over time, entitlement corrodes discipline, weakens leadership credibility, and drives high performers away from the very cultures meant to retain them.

Pay always communicates value even when leaders say nothing.

Error #2: Underpaying High Performers

Underpaying high performers is one of the most common and most underestimated compensation failures leaders make. It rarely feels urgent. Unlike overpaying underperformers, there is no immediate operational breakdown, no visible discipline issue, and no obvious cultural confrontation. Performance remains strong. Results continue. From the surface, everything appears stable.

That illusion is what makes this mistake dangerous.

High performers do not disengage loudly when they are underpaid. They disengage analytically. They continue to meet expectations while quietly re-evaluating the value exchange. They begin measuring effort against reward, responsibility against compensation, and contribution against recognition. When those calculations tilt out of balance, commitment erodes quietly.

This error often occurs for three reasons. First, compensation bands lag the market. Leadership intends to "review it next cycle," unaware that market alignment is time-sensitive, not annual. Second, raises are delayed due to budgetary caution, even as responsibilities expand. Output increases and expectations rise, yet pay remains static.

Third, leaders assume loyalty will compensate for misalignment. Culture, flexibility, and recognition are mistakenly treated as substitutes for equitable pay. They are not.

High performers are keenly aware of their value. They track their output, notice when peers are hired at comparable or higher rates, and understand what their skills command in the external market. When compensation does not reflect contribution, they do not immediately leave, but they begin comparing.

Underpayment does not prompt impulsive resignation. It prompts quiet validation.

The Controlled Contributor

A high-performing professional continues to deliver results but begins narrowing their efforts to their job descriptions. Initiative becomes selective. Discretionary effort declines. The employee still performs well—but no longer overperforms.

Leaders often misinterpret this shift as maturity or burnout. It is neither. It is recalibration.

Once the value exchange feels uneven, a high performer mentally revises the contract. They reduce emotional investment while maintaining output long enough to protect their reputation. Engagement turns transactional. Loyalty becomes conditional.

By the time external exploration begins, the decision is already half made.

The 8% Difference

A technology company lost a senior engineer to a competitor offering an 8% higher salary. Leadership believed employees would stay because the work-life balance was strong, the culture was positive, and recognition was frequent.

The exit interview revealed: "I loved working here. But I felt under-leveled financially."

Eight percent was not the issue. Perceived misalignment was.

The Small Gap Fallacy

Many leaders are surprised when high performers leave for seemingly minor pay increases. The mistake is focusing on the percentage rather than the signal it sends.

An eight percent increase rarely causes turnover. Perceived undervaluation does.

When compensation is not aligned with contribution, it sends a clear message: performance is appreciated but not valued enough to be protected.

Culture, recognition, and strong relationships delay departure, but they cannot override sustained misalignment. Pay legitimizes value. When it does not, trust erodes.

The Cultural Cost of Underpayment

While overpaying underperformers signals that standards don't matter, underpaying high performers sends a different, equally damaging message: Excellence is optional.

When top contributors realize their output isn't reflected proportionally in compensation, they adjust their behavior or leave. Remaining employees notice. Ambition softens. Standards flatten. High performance becomes a personal sacrifice rather than an organizational expectation.

Underpayment doesn't just lose talent. It normalizes mediocrity.

Compensation Compression: The Silent Resentment

Another form of underpaying high performers is compression. Organizations hire new talent at current market rates while long-term high performers remain on outdated compensation. The result is subtle yet corrosive.

Veterans notice when experience, institutional knowledge, and consistent delivery are compensated at the same level or below that of new hires. Leadership often avoids recalibration conversations to prevent discomfort, fueling resentment.

When loyalty is punished, stability becomes a liability rather than an asset.

Why Leaders Miss It

Leaders often rationalize underpayment because output continues. Results mask disengagement. Metrics remain intact. Culture appears positive. By the time compensation becomes a topic, the employee has already emotionally detached.

The danger is not that high performers speak up; it is that they no longer need to.

Exchange Value

When high performers are underpaid, compensation no longer reflects their value. Once the value exchange breaks, no amount of praise, culture, or flexibility can permanently restore trust. Pay doesn't buy loyalty, but misaligned pay eventually erodes it.

Retention fails when compensation does not reflect perceived contributions. Even small pay gaps signal undervaluation, and no amount of culture or recognition can override that signal.

The Compensation Compression Problem

Another trap arises when new hires are brought in at competitive market rates while long-term employees remain on outdated compensation. creating compression. Veterans notice when new employees earn salaries comparable to or higher than their own. If leadership does not proactively recalibrate, resentment builds. Transparency matters.

Pillar: Pay

When compensation is not recalibrated as the market shifts, compression turns loyalty into resentment, making transparency nonnegotiable.

The Cost of Misaligned Incentives

Incentives must drive the right behavior. Common bonus mistakes include rewarding revenue without margin discipline, incentivizing speed over quality, and rewarding output without collaboration. When bonuses misalign with strategy, behavior distorts. Compensation shapes decision-making.

Scenario: Incentive Distortion

The sales team receives compensation based solely on the amount they sell.

Results:

- Discounting increases
- Profit margins shrink
- Client retention declines

The compensation structure rewarded the wrong metric. Incentives are powerful. Design them carefully.

Executive-Level Compensation Oversight

Senior leaders must review compensation systems each year.

Ask:

1. Are high performers compensated in proportion to their performance?
2. Are underperformers protected by tenure?
3. Are incentives aligned with strategic goals?
4. Are pay structures market-aligned?

If compensation isn't reviewed on a regular basis, misalignment happens.

Pillar: Pay

When compensation systems aren't regularly reviewed, they can become outdated and cause problems.

The Discipline Conversation

Addressing compensation misalignment, like unequal pay or unfair bonus plans, requires courage because it often involves challenging established norms and advocating for change.

The manager began the discipline conversation by stating, "Your compensation reflects performance expectations that are not currently being met. We need to realign output to pay." The manager then outlined the specific performance gaps, clarified the standards that must be met, and reinforced that the purpose of the conversation was to reset expectations and ensure accountability moving forward.

This conversation may be uncomfortable but avoiding it can harm the culture more.

The Transparency Balance

Leaders must balance transparency with discretion. While individual salaries may remain private, the compensation structure should be clear—how progression works, which metrics matter, and what readiness requires. When progression criteria are known, perceptions of "fairness" increase.

This preserves the original language exactly, while improving readability and ensuring consistency with the pay discipline sections.

Pillar: Pay

Transparency in compensation builds trust, while secrecy in rules destroys it.

Compensation Discipline

Compensation discipline reflects leadership maturity. Pay should align with measurable value, be structured transparently, reviewed regularly, and enforced consistently. Strong pay systems foster high performance, address underperformance, and stabilize culture. As pay systems weaken, entitlement grows, frustration builds, and excellence quietly erodes.

Underpaying a high performer never looks like negligence; it looks like patience, caution, or fiscal responsibility. But when contribution outpaces compensation for too long, patience turns into exit planning. Overpaying underperformers is equally destructive. Financially protecting underperformance does not preserve loyalty; it penalizes performance. And when organizations reward comfort, tenure, or sentiment instead of current contribution, the culture pays the price.

Pay must keep pace with value, or value will eventually leave.

Reflection Audit – Chapter 8

1. Are any underperformers paid more than their contribution level?
2. Have high performers referenced market comparisons recently?
3. Are bonus incentives aligned with strategic goals?
4. When was the last full compensation review conducted?

If answers are unclear, misalignment might already be happening.

Leadership Shift

Effective leaders do not wait for compensation complaints to surface. They proactively audit pay alignment. They track performance growth relative to compensation growth. They recalibrate before resentment takes hold.

Correcting overpayment requires resolve. Leaders must realign roles, expectations, and compensation to reflect current contributions, not comfort, tenure, or sentiment. Difficult conversations preserve culture. Avoiding them sacrifices it.

Likewise, disciplined leaders recognize that underpaying high performers erodes trust long before it leads to resignation. They understand that fairness is not accidental, it is maintained. When compensation accurately and predictably reflects value, accountability strengthens, high performance becomes repeatable, and the culture stabilizes.

Strong leaders protect standards by maintaining alignment. Alignment begins with pay that reflects value.

Praise establishes standards. *Pay enforces them.*

Chapter 9

Incentives, Bonuses, and Performance Multipliers

Designing Pay Systems That Drive the Right Behavior

Incentives Shape Decisions

Every compensation structure answers a silent question: "What behavior does leadership want repeated?" If incentives are poorly designed, organizations unintentionally reward the wrong actions. When incentives are aligned strategically, performance increases significantly.

Incentives are directional tools. They not only compensate for effort but also influence priorities.

The Three Incentive Errors

Most organizations fall into one of three traps:

1. Overemphasizing short-term results
2. Rewarding individual output at the expense of collaboration
3. Incentivizing volume without quality

Each creates distortion.

The Sales Volume Collapse Incentive Design Failure Case

A mid-sized company adopted an aggressive quarterly bonus system based solely on sales volume. After two quarters, revenue grew, but discounting also increased, profit margins declined, and customer loss worsened. Sales reps are rewarded with commission rather than long-term sustainability. The structure emphasizes activity over strategic value.

Incentives drove behavior exactly as designed. Leadership shaped behavior in the wrong direction.

Effective incentives must reflect:

- Strategic priorities
- Balance short-term and long-term results
- Protect margin and quality
- Promote collaboration

Before implementing any incentive, ask: "What unintended behavior could this produce?" If you cannot answer that clearly, redesign it.

Short-Term vs Long-Term Motivation

Short-term incentives include quarterly bonuses, commissions, and spot bonuses which creates a sense of urgency. Long-term incentives include equity participation, profit sharing, and leadership track advancement, which drives loyalty. Short-term and long-term incentives should coexist, and focusing too much on one can disrupt the culture.

Scenario: Bonus Fatigue- Incentive Design Failure Case

A regional operations team received monthly performance bonuses linked to specific goals. Initially, productivity increased. After six months, output leveled off, motivation dropped, and complaints grew. Why? What was once a reward is now an expectation. Bonuses have lost their motivational power. Incentives need to adapt.

Incentive Design Standard -The Escalation Principle

If incentives remain unchanged, performance stalls. To prevent stagnation, incentive structures should gradually modify targets, introduce tiered bonuses, and link incentives to development milestones.

Progression sustains engagement. Static incentives create stagnation.

Incentive Design Success Case-The Tiered Performance Multiplier

A logistics company implemented a tiered bonus structure. Tier 1: achieved the standard target. Tier 2: exceeded the target by 10%. Tier 3: exceeded the target by 20% while maintaining quality benchmarks. The additional requirement of quality maintenance prevented shortcuts.

Results showed higher efficiency, lower error rates, and better collaboration. The incentive design promoted balanced behavior.

Incentivizing Collaboration

A common cause of incentive failure is over-rewarding individual achievements. When the focus is solely on personal metrics, it leads to information hoarding, heightened internal competition, and reduced knowledge sharing. Effective leaders integrate individual, team, and organizational performance metrics. Balanced incentives helps maintain a healthy company culture.

Dialogue Example: Commission Realignment

During the commission realignment discussion, the executive said, "Our current commission plan rewards volume. We're adjusting it to reward margin and retention." The sales lead responded, "That changes how we prioritize accounts." The executive replied, "That's the point." The exchange clarified that the organization was shifting from a quantity-driven model to a value-driven one, signaling that future compensation would be tied to profitable growth, customer longevity, and disciplined account management rather than raw activity.

Incentive Rule: Incentives must align with long-term sustainability.

Executive Compensation Philosophy

At senior levels, compensation must reflect strategic decision-making, organizational health, and long-term stability.

Linking executive bonuses solely to quarterly profits encourages short-term thinking.

Balanced executive incentives include:

- Multi-year performance metrics
- Culture health indicators
- Succession development progress

Leadership behavior follows compensation design.

Avoiding Reward Addiction

If employees expect constant bonus stimulation, intrinsic motivation weakens. Leaders must ensure recognition reinforces behavior, compensation legitimizes value, and incentives accelerate performance but do not replace accountability. Bonuses supplement the structure. They do not substitute discipline.

Consequences of Misaligned Incentives

Misaligned incentives do not fail quietly; they succeed in the wrong direction.

Diagnostic Reminder

- Praise reinforces standards.
- Pay accelerates measurable value.
- Position sustains long-term commitment.

Misaligned incentives occur when pay rewards the wrong outcome, or when pay is used where Praise or Position should lead.

Reflection Audit – Chapter 9

1. What behaviors are your incentives currently reinforcing?
2. Are margins protected in your compensation structure?
3. Do incentives align individual and team results?
4. Have targets remained static too long?
5. Are executive incentives aligned with long-term strategies?

If incentive structures are not reviewed within 12 months, issues may arise.

Leadership Shift

Incentives are not merely motivational tricks; they shape how organizations operate. When strategically designed, they boost performance, enhance quality, foster better collaboration, and strengthen loyalty. However, if misaligned, they can distort culture, encourage shortcuts, and lead to burnout among high performers.

Pay should be disciplined, and incentives must be carefully designed. Both are essential to maintaining the integrity of the Three P's of People Development model.

Praise sets standards. Pay accelerates value. Incentives work only when discipline leads.

Incentives don't motivate; they steer.

Chapter 9 aligns incentives with the behaviors you want repeated.

Chapter 10 shifts from pay to preparation for advancement.

PART IV - POSITION

ADVANCEMENT AS A LEADERSHIP STRATEGY

Chapter 10

Advancement Is Not Promotion - It is Preparation

The Most Expensive Leadership Mistake

Promoting without proper preparation can be one of the most harmful decisions an organization makes. It may seem rewarding, validating, and fair. However, when advancement depends solely on tenure, loyalty, or performance, it can lead to leadership instability. A position should be earned through proven skills and readiness not just effort.

The Promotion Myth

High performance in one role doesn't guarantee readiness for the next. Yet most companies rely on consistent results, longevity, dependability, and personal trust when making promotions. None of these factors guarantee leadership readiness. Advancement requires new skills, and without preparation, performance can decline at the next level.

Leadership Development Programs

Leadership development programs prepare individuals for promotion. Their purpose is to build the skills needed at the next level before assuming authority, not after performance declines. These programs should be intentional, well-organized, and aligned with the demands of leadership roles rather than with seniority or past achievements.

Effective leadership development emphasizes skill acquisition, decision-making ability, and behavioral readiness. Participation indicates potential, but completion alone does not ensure advancement. Promotion decisions should be based on demonstrated growth, applied learning, and sustained capability at the required level.

When leadership development programs are lacking, informal, or viewed as optional, organizations face a higher risk of role misalignment, declining performance, and leadership instability. When intentionally designed, they safeguard performance continuity and emphasize that leadership is a responsibility earned through preparation.

Policy Failure Analysis – The Assistant Manager's Collapse

1. Policy Context and Decision: A retail company promoted a top-performing assistant manager to store manager. The assistant manager was dependable, high-output, and customer-focused.

2. Observed Outcomes: After promotion, conflict avoidance increased, corrective conversations were delayed, and team standards declined. Within six months, turnover increased, revenue decreased, and morale declined.

3. Root Cause Determination: The issue was readiness. He had never received training in authority calibration, conflict resolution, or performance accountability.

4. Policy Failure Conclusion: Promotion occurred before preparation.

The Readiness Principle

The position requires demonstration of skills in decision-making under pressure, emotional regulation, conflict management, strategic thinking, and accountability enforcement. If any of these are underdeveloped, advancement must pause. Promotion without readiness harms the individual, the team, and the culture.

Scenario: The "Next in Line" Assumption

An employee is often seen as the "next in line' due to high performance, likability, and tenure. Leadership often assumes promotion will happen automatically without assessing their readiness. When promoted, any gaps in skills or leadership qualities become apparent. The organization often realizes too late that being well-liked does not necessarily mean they are ready to lead. A position should be earned by developing relevant skills.

The Leadership Readiness Pyramid

- At the base: Competence
- Above that: Emotional Maturity
- Above that: Authority
- At the top: Influence

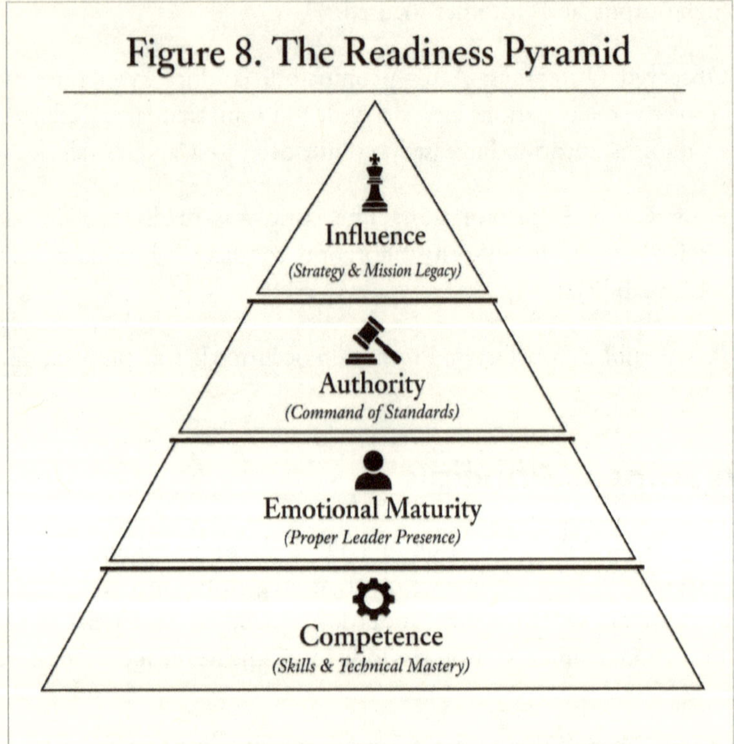

Competence without authority causes hesitation, authority without emotional intelligence breeds fear, and influence without accountability creates instability. Advancement must move through pathways. Skipping pathways causes collapse.

Policy Success Case -The Prepared Successor

A logistics company implemented structured development paths. Before being promoted to regional manager, candidates were required to lead cross-functional duties, manage budgets, conduct corrective performance conversations, and present strategy updates to executives. When promotions occurred, transitions were smooth because prepared leaders require less guidance. Proper preparation lowers risk.

Retention Policy Principle

Position-driven employees think long term, ask about growth pathways, seek visibility in strategic discussions, and volunteer for responsibility. If growth is unclear, they do not stagnate. They leave.

The Growth Visibility Strategy

To retain position-driven individuals, leaders must offer clear career pathways, established readiness milestones, transparent timelines, and development opportunities. Ambiguity leads to exit planning. Clarity encourages commitment.

Dialogue Example: The Advancement Conversation

During the advancement discussion, the employee said, “I want to move into leadership.” The manager responded, “Let’s define what leadership readiness looks like.” When the employee asked, “What does that include?” the manager replied, “Conflict management, strategic planning exposure, and accountability enforcement. We’ll map your progress over the next 12 months.” The scenario reinforces that advancement is not based on hope, tenure, or informal interest—it requires a defined set of measurable readiness criteria, a structured development path, and a clear timeline that aligns capability with responsibility.

Advancement becomes structured; it is not speculative.

Leadership Readiness Failure Pattern

The Authority Calibration Problem

Some newly promoted leaders struggle because they have not yet developed an authority mindset. They hesitate to correct peers, enforce standards, and make unpopular decisions. Advancement requires a shift in identity. Without coaching during this transition, leaders tend to revert to old habits. Psychological preparation is also necessary.

Succession is a System, not a Reaction

Strong organizations always know who is ready now, who will be ready in 12 months, and who needs development. If a vacancy causes panic, succession planning is weak. Position strategy safeguards organizational stability.

The Pillars of Advancement

Praise Engages

Recognizing and acknowledging achievements inspires motivation and commitment. When team members genuinely feel appreciated for their contributions, engagement increases. Praise acts as a catalyst, energizing individuals and encouraging them to invest more in their work.

Pay Aligns

Compensation reflects organizational values and priorities. When pay is aligned with performance and responsibilities, it reinforces expectations and fosters a culture of accountability. Fair and consistent pay promotes a sense of trust and clarity around advancement.

Position Sustains

Position provides lasting structure and stability. When advancement is based on readiness and measurable performance, it enhances leadership pipelines and organizational longevity. The right position, earned through preparation and merit, sustains both the culture and the team's ongoing effectiveness.

Reflection Audit – Chapter 10

1. Are promotions based on readiness or tenure?
2. Do you have documented readiness criteria?
3. Who on your team is position-driven?
4. Have you provided clear growth pathways?
5. If a leader resigns tomorrow, who is prepared to step in?

If the answers are uncertain, there is a risk of advancement.

Leadership Shift

A position is a responsibility, not a reward. Advancement should be based on preparation, readiness, and measurable performance metrics. When a position is earned strategically, leadership pipelines strengthen, retention improves, culture stabilizes, and organizational longevity increases. When a position is granted emotionally, performance destabilizes, teams fracture, and talent leaves. Praise engages. Pay aligns. Position sustains.

How can organizations create structured pathways for advancement that align with employee motivation?

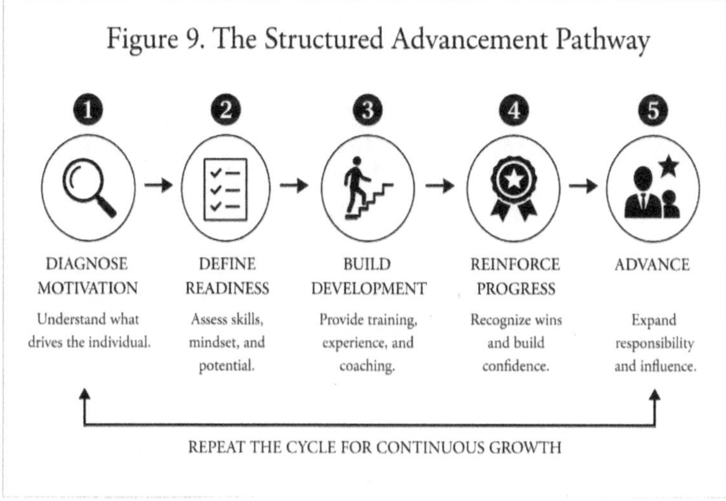

Figure 9. The Structured Advancement Pathway

Structured advancement pathways replace assumptions with clarity. When motivation is diagnosed, readiness is defined, and development is visible, advancement becomes predictable rather than political.

Advancement: preparation equals readiness and readiness equals measured promotion

Promotion without readiness is organizational debt.

Chapter 10 made advancement a preparation standard.

Chapter 11 builds the pipeline that sustains it.

Chapter 11

Building a Leadership Development Pipeline

Designing Predictable Growth – Not Accidental

The Reactive Leadership Trap

Many organizations respond reactively when a leader resigns. A vacancy arises, pressure mounts, and the executive team then asks, "Who can step in quickly?"

When leadership pipelines are weak, promotion becomes reactive not strategic. Reactivity leads to compromises which in turn creates instability. Succession must be planned well in advance of when it is needed.

The Pipeline Principle

Every organization should be able to answer three questions instantly:

1. Who is ready now?

2. Who will be ready in 12 months?

3. Who is being prepared for future leadership beyond that?

If those answers are unclear, the leadership pipeline is not fully developed. Leadership development should be visible and intentional.

The Multi-Unit Expansion

A regional retail store is planned to open five new locations within two years. However, an internal review found that no assistant managers had been trained in multi-unit management, that financial literacy training was inconsistent, and that exposure to conflict management was limited. Consequently, the expansion was delayed. Leadership capacity, not capital, was the real constraint.

The company implemented rotational leadership assignments, budget management training, and exposure to strategic planning. Within 18 months, five internal promotions were made. Preparation fuels growth.

Expansion should never outpace leadership readiness.

The Leadership Exposure Model

Leadership readiness requires exposure beyond the current scope. High-potential employees must participate in cross-functional collaboration, budget management, performance improvement, strategic planning meetings, and communicate effectively with senior leadership.

Promotion is experimental without exposure and measurable with it.

Scenario: Developmental Assignment Design

A high-performing supervisor shows interest in advancement. Instead of promising a future promotion, you assign cross-team responsibilities, ownership of the quarterly performance review process, and direct management of a small project budget.

Developmental assignments showcase decision-making maturity, emotional control, accountability, and strategic thinking.

The Readiness Scorecard

Every organization should create a readiness scorecard that includes competence, emotional maturity, the application of authority, and strategic thinking. Competence encompasses operational skills and process understanding. Emotional maturity involves conflict resolution and openness to coaching.

The application of authority requires a willingness to enforce standards and to be comfortable making tough decisions. Strategic thinking includes long-term planning and situational awareness. Scorecards help ensure that promotions are based on more than past performance.

The Pipeline Ladder

A structured leadership ladder might consist of entry-level, supervisor, team lead, senior manager, director, and executive roles.

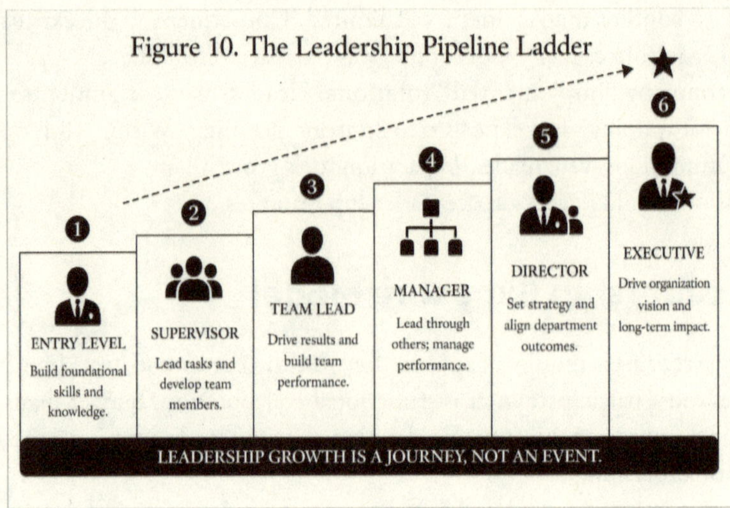

Each level must have documented competencies, clearly defined responsibilities, measurable readiness milestones, and specific experience requirements.

Without documentation, advancement appears subjective, creating a perception of favoritism.

The Hidden High-Potential

A manufacturing plant overlooked a quiet engineer for years because she did not showcase her expertise. During a structured "pipeline" review, her cross-functional influence was highlighted. She was assigned to lead an initiative to optimize efficiency across departments.

She advanced to an operations leadership role within a year. Her performance demonstrated outstanding strategic thinking. The Pipeline ladder reveals talent that personality-driven leadership might overlook.

Rule: Leadership pipelines uncover potential that visibility alone cannot.

Preventing Leadership Bottlenecks

Pipeline stagnation occurs when:

1. Senior leaders resist delegating authority.

2. Advancement criteria are unclear.

3. Exposure opportunities are limited.

4. Performance metrics overshadow development metrics.

When leaders hoard authority, pipelines stall. Succession should be intentional.

Dialogue Example: Structured Development Conversation

The manager said, "You've expressed interest in leadership. Here's the readiness structure. Over the next 12 months, we'll evaluate you across these four categories." The employee asked, "What will that look like in practice?" The manager replied, "You'll lead a cross-functional project, manage a small budget, and conduct corrective conversations with coaching support."

Clarity reduces ambiguity and ambiguity reduces commitment.

Development Timelines

Leadership pipelines must include time expectations. *For example:*

- 6 months – developmental assignment

- 12 months – readiness evaluation

- 18 months – promotion eligibility review

Timelines provide motivation, whereas undefined timelines create frustration.

The Organizational Stability Benefit

When pipelines are strong:

1. Resignations cause minimal disruption.

2. Internal promotions increase.

3. Institutional knowledge remains.

4. Culture strengthens.

The result: A well-planned position strategy reduces chaos.

Reflection Audit – Chapter 11

1. Is there a documented leadership ladder?

2. Do readiness scorecards exist?

3. Are high-potential employees receiving exposure?

4. Are advancement timelines visible?

5. Can you fill a leadership vacancy tomorrow?

If not, the pipeline requires development.

Leadership Shift

Leadership pipelines fail not because talent is missing but because preparation is inconsistent. Organizations that lose momentum during growth face repeated leadership disruptions. They rarely lack capable people; they lack a disciplined system to develop them. When advancement depends on urgency, tenure, or trust rather than readiness, succession becomes reactive and the culture fragile.

The leadership shift in this chapter is from reactive replacement to intentional preparation. Strong leaders do not wait for vacancies to ask who is ready; they always know. They build pipelines that make readiness visible long before promotion decisions are required. When preparation is ongoing, promotion becomes confirmation, not correction.

A leadership pipeline is not a list of names; it is a system of exposure, assessment, and development. It answers three questions continuously: who is ready now, who is developing toward readiness, and which skills are still missing. When leaders cannot answer those questions clearly, advancement becomes speculative and risk increases. Stability is not created by loyalty, it is created by preparedness.

This shift requires leaders to stop treating development as optional and start treating it as structural. High-potential employees do not disengage because they lack ambition; they disengage when growth is invisible. When exposure, readiness standards, and timelines are unclear, position-driven talent interprets silence as a ceiling. A visible pipeline turns uncertainty into commitment by making progression measurable and attainable.

Effective leaders also recognize that pipelines protect more than promotions, they protect performance. Prepared leaders transition faster, require less correction, and uphold standards consistently. Unprepared leaders consume time, weaken accountability, and destabilize teams. Every promotion without preparation creates hidden organizational debt. Every prepared promotion strengthens continuity.

The leadership mandate is clear: stop relying on personal judgment alone and start building repeatable systems. Document readiness criteria. Create developmental assignments. Publish timelines. Review pipelines regularly. When preparation is intentional, succession becomes predictable, expansion becomes sustainable, and leaders step into roles ready to perform; not discover expectations after the fact.

- Pipelines do not accelerate growth by chance, they sustain it by design.
- When development is visible, advancement becomes credible.
- When readiness is measured, promotion becomes stable.
- And when leadership capacity is prepared in advance, the organization stops reacting and starts enduring.

Growth is fragile without a pipeline; sustainable with one.

Chapter 12

Integrating the Three P's

Designing a Culture Where Motivation is Aligned - Not Assumed

The Danger of Isolated Strategy

Some organizations focus heavily on praise, others on pay, and some on position, with very few combining all three. Integration fosters stability.

When one P dominates, the culture distorts:

- Praise without Pay feels symbolic.
- Pay without Position feels transactional.
- Position without Praise feels political.

The Alignment Model

Think of it in layers: Praise builds confidence; pay fosters accountability; and position shapes future vision.

When layered properly, recognition increases effort, compensation affirms it, and advancement sustains it. Remove one, and motivation declines over time.

The One - Dimensional Culture

A startup fostered a strong culture of praise, with founders publicly celebrating innovation each week. Team morale stayed high. However, the compensation structure was inconsistent.

Promotion criteria were unclear. After two years, senior engineers departed for more structured organizations. Growth stalled. While praise created excitement, the lack of pay discipline and unclear roles caused instability.

The Transactional Corporation

A sales organization had a clear commission structure, and compensation was transparent. Bonuses were generous, but recognition was scarce.

Development pathways were limited, and although sales numbers stayed strong, turnover remained high. Employees described the culture as "efficient but cold." Pay without praise weakens loyalty.

The Political Advancement Model

A family-owned business promoted internally, based on trust and longevity. While the importance of positions was emphasized, recognition was inconsistent, and compensation structures were outdated. Internal resentment grew, and high performers believed that career advancement was subjective. A position without pay and praise fosters the perception of favoritism.

The Integrated Leadership Equation

Sustainable motivation requires: Recognition plus measurable compensation plus visible growth pathways

All three must align with standards. When integrated, high performers feel recognized, the value exchange feels fair, career growth feels achievable, and retention stabilizes.

Scenario: Diagnosing a Department

A department reports declining engagement. Before acting, leadership must ask:

- Is recognition specific and consistent?
- Is compensation aligned with contribution?
- Are growth pathways visible?

If only one driver is adjusted, misalignment persists. Integration requires coordinated action.

The Career Stage Calibration

The dominance of each P may shift across career stages:

1. *Early Career*: praise-heavy + growth exposure

2. *Mid-Career:* balanced pay plus position clarity

3. *Senior Leadership:* position plus legacy alignment plus long-term incentives

Integration requires calibration, not uniformity.

Dialogue Example: Integrated Development Conversation

The manager said, "You've delivered a strong performance this year. We've publicly recognized that. Let's discuss compensation alignment and outline your growth pathway for next year." The employee replied, "That helps me see the bigger picture."

That single conversation integrates all three P's. Clarity boosts commitment.

Organizational Integration Checklist

To scale the integration of **Praise, Pay, and Position**:

1. Document recognition standards.

2. Define compensation tiers with measurable criteria.

3. Publish advancement readiness structures.

4. Review alignment annually.

5. Train managers in diagnostic conversations.

Integration must be systematic, not occasional.

Diagnosing Engagement Through the Three P's-Praise, Pay, Position

Performance metrics show results. Engagement indicators show sustainability. Employees can meet goals yet still be disengaged. To understand engagement, leaders must observe **behavioral signals and participation patterns**, not just output.

Figure 11. Engagement Indicators Model

INDICATOR	WHAT LEADERS OBSERVE	PRIMARY DRIVER	MISALIGNMENT SIGNAL
HIGH ENGAGEMENT	Enthusiastic, proactive, seeks challenges	Praise	Lack of recognition or appreciation
TRANSACTIONAL ENGAGEMENT	Consistent, goal-focused, asks about pay	Pay	Feels underpaid or compensation is unfair
DEVELOPMENT ENGAGEMENT	Asks about growth, seeks feedback	Position	Limited advancement or growth opportunities
DISENGAGEMENT	Withdrawn, quiet, minimal effort	All Three	Misalignment across one or more drivers

Engagement indicators often shift before performance declines or resignations occur.

Engagement strengthens when **Praise, Pay, and Position** align with the individual's motivation. When they are misaligned, engagement erodes quietly, even among high performers.

Performance measures output, whereas engagement measures longevity. Leaders who track engagement signals early can correct misalignment before results or retention are affected.

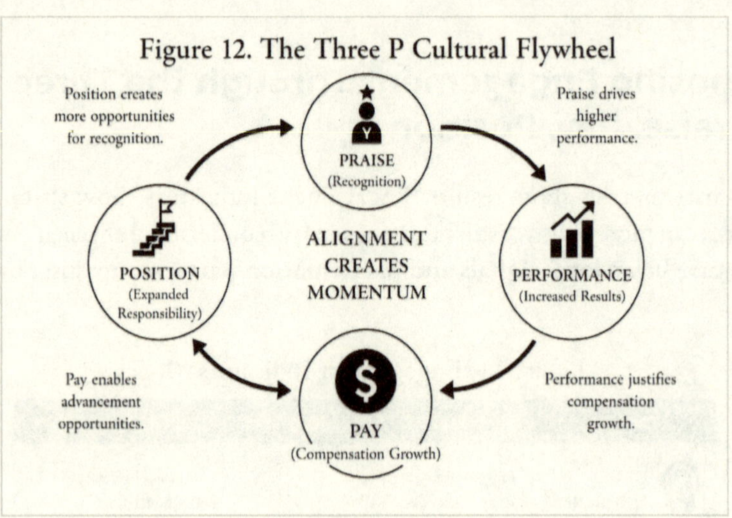

When the Three Align:

- Praise: Recognition
- Position: Increased Performance
- Pay: Compensation Growth
- Position: Expanded Responsibility
- Praise: Recognition

The cycle reinforces itself; when misaligned, the cycle reverses.

Diagnosing Engagement: Why Managers Must Learn to Ask Better Questions

A lack of effort, compensation, or opportunity does not cause most engagement failures. They are caused by misalignment.

Managers often respond to disengagement by increasing praise, adjusting pay, or offering advancement—without first understanding what is actually driving the individual. When the wrong driver is applied, engagement does not improve. It erodes quietly.

This is why engagement does not fail loudly. It fades through silence, reduced initiative, and emotional withdrawal—often while performance remains intact.

Effective leaders do not react to symptoms. They diagnose motivation.

Why Engagement Requires Diagnosis, Not Assumption

Praise, Pay, and Position are powerful drivers but only when applied accurately. Each individual responds differently, and these drivers change over time. Without diagnosis, even well intentioned leadership becomes random.

A manager who assumes everyone is pay-driven will use compensation to solve growth problems, and a manager who assumes everyone wants advancement will assign responsibility when recognition is what's actually needed. Both approaches feel active, but neither is effective. The issue isn't the action itself; it's acting without understanding what truly motivates the person.

What Diagnostic Conversations Do Differently

Diagnostic conversations are not check-ins, performance reviews, or coaching sessions. They are structured leadership conversations that uncover what currently drives engagement.

They require managers to:

- Observe patterns before acting
- Listen for what is repeated, not what is loudest
- Confirm the dominant driver instead of guessing

When managers diagnose accurately, leadership responses become precise. Praise reinforces the right behaviors. Pay clarifies value exchange. Position creates visible pathways.

Engagement stabilizes because they respond correctly.

Why This Skill Must Be Trained

Diagnostic skill does not develop from experience alone. Without structure, managers default to their own preferences, assumptions, or emotional reactions.

Organizations that want consistent engagement must therefore train managers to diagnose.

This capability cannot exist in theory alone. It must be practiced, reinforced, and supported by tools that help leaders observe, diagnose, and respond intentionally.

Table 3. Engagement Indicators Beyond Performance Metrics

INDICATOR	WHAT IT MEASURES	WHY IT MATTERS	EXAMPLES
SENSE OF PURPOSE	The degree to which employees feel their work is meaningful and aligned with the organization's mission.	Purpose drives intrinsic motivation and long-term commitment.	"I understand how my work contributes to the bigger picture."
RELATIONSHIP QUALITY	The strength of interpersonal connections and trust among team members and leaders.	Strong relationships improve collaboration, engagement, and retention.	Trust in leadership, peer support, team cohesion.
GROWTH MINDSET	The extent to which employees believe they can learn, grow, and develop in their roles.	A growth mindset fosters resilience, adaptability, and continuous improvement.	Openness to feedback, learning new skills, seeking challenges.
VOICE & INFLUENCE	The level of employee empowerment to speak up and influence decisions.	When people are heard, they feel valued and more committed.	Employees feel their opinions matter, ideas are considered, concerns are addressed.
WORK-LIFE BALANCE	The ability of employees to manage their work and personal life effectively.	Balance reduces burnout and supports sustainable engagement.	Flexible work options, manageable workload, respect for personal time.
PSYCHOLOGICAL SAFETY	The perception of being safe to take risks, ask questions, and admit mistakes.	Safety encourages innovation, honesty, and team learning.	Comfort speaking up, no fear of blame, mistakes seen as learning opportunities.

Reflection Audit – Chapter 12

1. Which P is strongest in your organization?
2. Which P is weakest?
3. Are managers trained to diagnose motivational drivers?
4. Is alignment reviewed annually?
5. Does the leadership model integrate?

If integration is weak, retention will fluctuate.

Leadership Shift

Praise, Pay, and **Position** are not isolated tools; they form a ecosystem. When leaders integrate them, motivation becomes consistent, retention becomes strategic, development becomes measurable, and culture becomes resilient. Leadership maturity is not about choosing one driver; it is about sequencing all three.

An isolated strategy always distorts. Praise without **pay** becomes symbolic. Pay without position becomes transactional. Position without praise becomes political. Integration protects standards by aligning reinforcement, exchange, and advancement. Performance matters, fairness is real, and the future is visible.

The leadership shift is in discipline: diagnose the dominant driver, apply the right driver, then deliberately connect it to the other two drivers to ensure alignment holds over time. Integration is not a one-time initiative; it is a review rhythm. Chapter 13 turns this ecosystem into an executable 30–60–90 plan.

> *Leadership maturity is not about choosing one driver; it is about sequencing all three.*

Alignment fails when the pillars operate in isolation.

Chapter 12 integrates Praise, Pay, and Position into one operating model.

Chapter 13 turns the model into a rollout plan.

PART V - EXECUTIVE IMPLEMENTATION

TURNING THE THREE P's INTO ORGANIZATIONAL STRATEGY

Chapter 13

The 30-60-90 Day Rollout Plan

Moving From Concept to Culture

Implementation Without Structure Fails

Most leadership initiatives fail not because the idea is flawed, but because execution is inconsistent. Leaders read, agree, and intend to change, yet intention without structure falls apart. As the previous chapters have shown, motivation cannot be applied emotionally, development cannot be left to chance, and alignment cannot depend solely on individual effort.

The Three P's of People Development must be applied intentionally through disciplined systems that turn insight into steady action.

Phase One: 30 Days - Diagnose and Stabilize

Objective: Ensure clarity

Leadership Alignment

Bring senior leaders together to build a shared understanding of praise, pay, and position. Review current recognition practices, compensation, and career advancement pathways to identify strengths, gaps, and misalignments.

Organizational Diagnosis

Conduct an organizational diagnosis to assess how motivation is reinforced, rewarded, and fostered across departments. Identify areas where decisions are based on assumptions rather than data.

Talent Risk Identification

Identify top performers and understand their primary motivational drivers. Clarify where misalignment creates retention risks. A clear understanding reveals these risks. Proper diagnosis prevents errors.

Phase Two: 60 Days - Structure and Clarify

Objective: Build systems

Recognition System

Establish a weekly performance acknowledgment routine that clearly defines standards and is easy to replicate. Train managers on the specific language to use and on how to link recognition to measurable results.

Compensation Clarification

Document compensation levels to eliminate ambiguity and ensure raises are based on measurable value. Schedule structured performance reviews so compensation reflects contribution rather than emotion or tenure.

Advancement Structure

Publish the leadership ladder and define readiness scorecards to make growth requirements explicit. Introduce developmental assignments that allow leaders to observe capability before promotion.

- *Result:* Clarity lowers anxiety. Structure boosts commitment.
- *Transition*: (Structure to Stability)

Once expectations are clear and systems are defined, leadership discipline shifts from building alignment to sustaining it.

Phase Three: 90 Days - Reinforce and Adjust

Objective: Stabilize culture.

Measure Impact

Track engagement indicators, voluntary turnover, internal promotion rate, and performance metrics. Focus on trends over time rather than short-term perfection to stay aligned.

Correct Compensation Misalignment

When recognition weakens, retrain managers to reinforce standards more clearly. When compensation concerns persist, reevaluate transparency and alignment with value. When advancement remains unclear, be more transparent about your readiness criteria and career growth pathways.

Result: Standards are maintained. Adjustments safeguard culture. Diagnosis provides clarity. Structure ensures alignment. Reinforcement sustains culture.

Praise, Pay, and Position are more than steps in a process; they represent an operational discipline. When leaders diagnose accurately, systemize intentionally, and reinforce consistently, motivation becomes predictable, retention becomes strategic, development becomes measurable, and culture becomes resilient.

Reflection Audit – Chapter 13

In the past 30 days, did you diagnose the dominant driver (Praise, Pay, or Position) based on evidence—or on assumption?

1. Which part of your current approach relies on individual manager personalities rather than a repeatable system?

2. Where is recognition occurring without measurable standards, creating noise instead of reinforcement?

3. Which compensation rule is still unclear enough that managers will improvise—creating inconsistency by default?

4. Which growth pathway or readiness standard needs to be published so high-potential talent can see a future?

What will you measure at Day 90 to confirm the Three P's are being reinforced, not just discussed (turnover risk, engagement signals, internal promotions, performance)?

If the rollout can't be repeated without you, it isn't a system yet. Diagnose, align, reinforce, sustain.

Leadership Shift

Execution is not a motivational event; it is an operating rhythm. The Three P's create cultural stability only when leaders translate them into repeatable habits: diagnosis, alignment, reinforcement, and review.

The 30–60–90 plan protects against the most common leadership failure: inconsistency. In the first 30 days, leaders stop guessing and start diagnosing. In the next 60 days, they remove ambiguity by documenting standards and rules. In the final 90 days, they reinforce the right behaviors until the organization can feel the change without being told.

A rollout is successful when it changes what managers do on ordinary days: recognize, reward, and develop. When Praise reinforces standards, pay reflects measurable value, and position makes the future visible, motivation becomes predictable and culture becomes durable.

A model becomes culture only when it becomes a cadence.

Execution is where leadership models succeed—or disappear.

Chapter 13 moved from concept to culture.

Chapter 14 reinforces the diagnose–align–stabilize rhythm.

Chapter 14

The 30-60-90 Day Engagement Alignment

FIRST 30 DAYS - DIAGNOSE

Objective: Ensure Clarity

- Track engagement signals for individuals and the team.
- Identify which P **(Praise, Pay, Position)** is most active.
- Note early warning signs (silence, reduced initiative, fewer questions)

Result: A breakdown of baseline engagement levels by department

NEXT 60 DAYS - ALIGN

Objective: Correct misalignment

- Adjust recognition when praise is insufficient
- Explain how compensation works when pay is questioned.
- Make growth pathways clear when position is uncertain.

Result: Targeted actions for alignment by **Praise, Pay, or Position**

FINAL 90 DAYS - STABILIZE

Objective: Sustain engagement

- Reinforce behaviors that meet standards.

- Track changes in discretionary effort and communication.
- Confirm that engagement indicators improve before results change.

Result: Improved engagement stability and reduced retention risk.

Reflection Audit – Chapter 14

1. In the last 30 days, what signals show engagement is rising or eroding before performance changes?
2. Which P (Praise, Pay, Position) is currently the primary friction point in your team or department?
3. What is one alignment action you can execute in 60 days that removes ambiguity for your top performers?
4. What are you reinforcing in the final 90 days and how will you measure whether it is sticking?

If you can't name the signals, the driver, and the next action, alignment is not yet operational.

Leadership Shift

Engagement does not improve through intent; it improves through a cadence. Leaders who stabilize teams do three things consistently: they diagnose early signals, align the dominant driver, and reinforce what they want repeated.

The mistake is waiting for performance to decline before acting. Engagement deteriorates first through silence, reduced initiative, and withdrawal. The 30-60-90 alignment rhythm is a leadership discipline that forces action while you still have influence.

When leaders treat alignment as a cycle not a one-time fix, retention becomes predictable, accountability becomes clearer, and culture stops drifting. **Diagnose. Align. Stabilize**. Then repeat.

> ***Diagnose the driver.*** *Align Praise, Pay, and Position; then reinforce what you want repeated.*

What gets audited gets protected.

Chapter 15 makes alignment measurable.

Chapter 16 makes it adaptable by department.

Chapter 15

Organizational Audit

Measuring Alignment

The Annual Alignment Audit

Every organization should conduct an annual alignment review to foster responsibility and motivate leaders to remain proactive, since misalignment is unavoidable without one.

Praise Audit

- Is recognition tied to standards?
- Is it consistent across departments?
- Are high performers visibly acknowledged?

Pay Audit

- Are compensation ranges market-aligned?
- Are raises tied to measurable value?
- Are pay gaps decreasing too quickly?

Position Audit

- Are the readiness criteria clear?

- Are advancement pathways documented?
- Are high potentials identified?
- Are succession candidates visible?

Reflection Audit – Chapter 15

1. If you audited your organization today, which pillar would score lowest: Praise, Pay, or Position?
2. Where is performance being reinforced - rewarded or advanced?
3. Which compensation rules are unclear to managers (tiers, criteria, timing), creating inconsistency by default?
4. Where are readiness criteria absent, outdated, or ignored, forcing promotion decisions to become emotional or political?
5. What will you review quarterly to prevent drift (recognition cadence, pay alignment, pipeline readiness)?

What gets reviewed gets maintained; what isn't measured quietly degrades.

Leadership Shift

Leadership audit is not bureaucracy; it is protection. Cultures do not fail from a single bad decision; they fail from uncorrected drift.

When praise is inconsistent, standards become emotional. When pay is unclear, fairness becomes a rumor. When position is vague, ambition becomes external exploration. The audit makes these failure points visible early, while correction is still simple.

An executive team's job is not to be optimistic about culture; it is to be accurate about it. What gets reviewed gets maintained, and what gets ignored becomes the next resignation trend.

When Praise, Pay, and Position aren't reviewed, they drift.

Chapter 16

Department-Level Alignment Guide

Customizing Praise, Pay, and Position

Purpose of Department-Level Alignment

The Three P's of People Development operate at the individual level, but alignment is maintained at the department level. Departments differ in how they recognize, pay, and provide opportunities for advancement.

When leaders apply a single approach to all departments, misalignment can occur. This often leads to decreased engagement, higher turnover, and inconsistent performance not because of leadership's intentions, but because the primary motivational driver is misidentified.

This chapter provides a diagnostic guide to aligning **Praise, Pay,** and **Position** across departmental functions.

Department-level alignment is where the model becomes operational. The organization may have one set of values, but departments live in different realities: standards, different pressures, forms of effort, and definitions of "good." Calibration ensures that leaders reinforce the right behaviors in the environments where those behaviors are produced.

Without this calibration, leaders default to the same errors at scale: they use pay to solve recognition gaps, they use praise to avoid pay conversations, and they use position as a retention tool before readiness exists. The result is predictable—one department becomes transactional, another becomes politically driven, and another becomes disengaged despite strong performance.

Practically, department-level alignment means translating the Three P's into local clarity: the standards that matter most, the metrics that prove them, the reinforcement rhythm that keeps them visible, the pay rules that remove ambiguity, and the pathways that make growth believable. Once those elements are defined, leaders can diagnose faster and intervene earlier which is why the next step is to assess the dominant driver in each department.

Departmental Driver Assessment

Before implementing any strategy, leaders should identify the primary motivational driver in each department. Use the following assessment questions:

- How is performance measured in this department?
- Where is effort primarily focused—output, accuracy, emotional labor, or strategy?
- What are the most common questions performers ask?
- At what point does disengagement first become evident?

Departments are often driven by a single primary driver, but an individual diagnosis remains essential.

Department- Specific Alignment Rules

Sales Departments

Dominant Drivers: **Pay, Position**

Sales performance is results-driven, competitive, and measurable. Motivation centers on clear compensation and opportunities for advancement.

Alignment Indicators

Compensation should be closely linked to measurable results.

Incentives should support strategic priorities, not just volume.

Advancement criteria should be well documented and accessible to ensure transparency.

Recognition should emphasize results and discipline, not just effort.

Misalignment Indicators

Strong results with rising external exploration

Pay questions without clear answers

High performers plateauing without advancement discussions

Customer Service Departments

Dominant Drivers: Praise, Position

Customer service roles impose significant emotional demands on employees. Effective engagement is fueled by recognizing emotional labor, acknowledging it regularly and specifically in line with service standards, and offering clear, achievable development pathways.

Alignment Indicators

- Recognition must be frequent, specific, and tied to service standards
- Emotional labor should be acknowledged alongside metrics
- Development paths must be visible and attainable
- Compensation should reinforce stability, not act as the primary driver

Misalignment Indicators

- Sustained performance with rising emotional exhaustion
- Consistent attendance accompanied by withdrawal from engagement behaviors
- Decline in voluntary contribution, initiative, or problem-solving beyond role scope

Operations Departments

Dominant Drivers: Pay, Praise

Operations teams are motivated by pay and praise, with process leadership serving as a supporting motivator. They prioritize consistency, fairness, and clarity, expecting compensation and recognition to be directly linked to current contributions and established service standards. Recognition should focus on accuracy, efficiency, and discipline, ensuring advancement is based on readiness and process ownership rather than reliability alone.

Alignment Indicators

- Pay should reflect current contribution, not tenure
- Recognition should reinforce accuracy, efficiency, and discipline
- Leadership roles should be tied to process ownership
- Advancement should follow readiness, not reliability alone

Misalignment Indicators

- Resentment toward compensation decisions
- High standards without reinforcement (recognition)
- Overpaid underperformance tolerated

Technical and Professional Departments (IT, Engineering, Finance)

Dominant Drivers: Position, Pay

In technical and professional departments such as IT, Engineering, and Finance, position and pay are the primary motivators. Compensation should accurately reflect both market value and individual contributions, rather than simply rewarding tenure or reliability. Recognition should highlight attributes such as impact, problem-solving skills, and expertise, while reinforcing high standards of accuracy, efficiency, and discipline. Leadership opportunities must be connected to process ownership, and advancement should be based on readiness and proven experience in strategic work, not just consistency. Clear career pathways, including both technical and leadership tracks, are essential for alignment, whereas misalignment is often indicated by resentment toward compensation decisions, tolerance for underperformance, and ambiguity about advancement.

Alignment Indicators

- Career pathways should be clearly defined, including technical and leadership tracks.
- Compensation should match market value and individual contributions.
- Recognition should emphasize impact, problem-solving, and expertise.
- Gaining experience in strategic work should come before seeking advancement.

Misalignment Indicators

- Lateral exits with small pay differences
- Advancement ambiguity
- View recognition as superficial.

Executive Teams

Dominant Drivers: Position, Pay

Executive teams are mainly driven by position and pay, with promotion and recognition closely tied to their leadership decisions and responsibilities. For genuine alignment, incentives should encourage long-term organizational behavior and pay must mirror both the responsibilities they hold and the risks they take on. Recognition works best when it supports sound decision-making and disciplined leadership.

Alignment Indicators

- Incentives must align with long-term organizational health.
- Succession development must be measured and reinforced.
- Compensation should reflect responsibility and risk

- Praise should reinforce decision quality and leadership discipline

Misalignment Indicators

- Short-term decision bias
- Weak leadership pipelines
- Tolerance of misalignment at senior levels

Department -Level Alignment Audit

Leaders should review each department annually using the following:

Praise Audit

- Is recognition consistent and standards-based?
- Is effort acknowledged where emotional labor exists?
- Are high performers visibly reinforced?

Pay Audit

- Does compensation accurately reflect current contributions?
- Are pay structures transparent?
- Are high performers undervalued or undercompensated?

Position Audit

- Are development pathways documented?
- Are the readiness criteria clear?
- Is succession planning proactive?

Failure in any category signals a risk of misalignment.

Leadership Risk Misalignment

When departments consistently misuse **Praise**, **Pay**, or **Position** for example, using praise to address compensation gaps or advancing employees before they are ready misalignment grows throughout the organization. This turns what could be isolated retention problems into widespread, systemic risks.

Using:

- Pay to solve recognition gaps
- Praise for resolving compensation issues
- Position without proper readiness

Causes instability, rather than engagement.

Reflection Audit – Chapter 16

1. Which department is being led uniformity rather than calibrated and what is it costing you (turnover, quality, speed, trust)?
2. Where are leaders using pay to solve a praise problem, or using praise to avoid a pay problem?
3. In each major department, what is the dominant driver and what evidence supports that conclusion?
4. Which department needs a clearer pathway (position) more than a higher incentive?
5. What is one adjustment you can implement this quarter to improve alignment without increasing budget?

Leadership Shift

Department leadership requires precision, not uniformity.

Consistency is maintained by matching the right driver to the right motivation, not by treating all departments uniformly.

When departmental alignment is correct:

- Engagement stabilizes
- Performance becomes predictable

- Retention strengthens
- Culture matures

Calibration is a leadership discipline: the same model, applied differently by context.

Calibration helps avoid imbalance; protects performance across functions.

Uniformity is easy; calibration is leadership.

Chapter 16 translated the model at the department level.

Chapter 17 elevates it to CEO-level strategy.

Chapter 17

CEO-Level Strategy

Leading the Praise, Pay, Position Ecosystem

Executive Responsibility

CEOs must ensure that recognition standards are consistent, that the approach to compensation is grounded in a structured philosophy, and that succession planning remains proactive, inspiring a sense of purpose and accountability across leadership levels. Integration should be demonstrated at the executive level.

Leadership Tolerance Test

If the CEO accepts overpaid underperformance, unrecognized excellence, and promotes without readiness, the organization will reflect this behavior. Culture follows leadership tolerance.

Reflection Audit – Chapter 17

1. What behaviors are currently tolerated at senior levels that would be unacceptable elsewhere in the organization?

2. Where is excellence being produced but not visibly reinforced by the executive team?

3. Which compensation misalignment is most likely to create executive-level drift (overpaying underperformance, compression, or misaligned incentives)?

4. If a key leader resigned today, is succession truly ready or merely assumed?

5. What is the one executive standard you will reinforce publicly within the next 30 days?

At the top, alignment is demonstrated not declared.

Leadership Shift

At the CEO level, the Three P's are not concepts; they are controls. Recognition, compensation, and advancement shape what leaders prioritize, tolerate, and repeat.

Culture follows what the executive team rewards and permits. If underperformance is financially protected, standards soften. If excellence is not reinforced, top talent detaches. If succession is assumed rather than measured, continuity becomes fragile.

CEO-level alignment is shown in decisions that keep the ecosystem disciplined: standards are visible, pay reflects value, and readiness is audited. When the top is aligned, the organization stops guessing and starts executing. At the top, tolerance becomes policy. What leadership permits, the organization repeats.

At the CEO level, praise sets standards, pay enforces them, and position protects the future.

Culture follows what the CEO tolerates.

Chapter 17 clarified executive accountability for the ecosystem.

Chapter 18 delivers the leadership charge.

Chapter 18

The Leadership Charge

Intentional Development Wins

People don't leave randomly. They leave when recognition is missing, compensation is misaligned, and growth opportunities are unclear. A lack of effort doesn't cause these issues; they stem from misalignment.

Providing leaders with clear guidance:

- Boost performance and conduct with praise
- Validate contribution and value with pay
- Drive growth by highlighting opportunities and providing clear direction with position.

Leadership isn't just about managing tasks; it's about intentionally developing people.

When leaders use praise, pay, and position strategically:

- Engagement stabilizes
- Retention is strengthens
- Succession begins to feel predictable
- Culture matures

Motivation is not mysterious; it can be measured with diagnostic tools and assessments. Alignment is a data-driven decision that helps leaders apply the Three P's-**Praise**, **Pay**, **Position** to enhance motivation, retention, and organizational culture.

Reflection Audit – Chapter 18

1. Which single misalignment (Praise, Pay, or Position) is most likely to cost you your best people this year?
2. What is one leadership behavior you will stop tolerating immediately because it weakens standards?
3. What is one reinforcement habit you will implement weekly to make expectations visible?
4. What is one compensation rule you will clarify so managers stop improvising?
5. What is one advancement pathway you will document so high-potential talent can see a future?

The model works when it becomes a cadence; diagnose, align, reinforce, and sustain.

Leadership Shift

The Three P's only work when they become leadership habits. Praise must reinforce standards. Pay must reflect measurable value. Position must make the future visible.

Your culture will not hold itself. If leaders do not diagnose, align, and reinforce on purpose, teams will drift by default and high performers will interpret that drift as the absence of a future.

The charge is simple: stop guessing. Build the cadence. Make standards visible, keep exchange fair, and make growth explicit. That is how motivation becomes stable and how retention becomes earned.

> ***Culture does not hold itself.*** *Leaders either build the cadence, or the organization drifts.*

CONCLUSION

The Three P's of People Development is built on a simple truth: people do not disengage because they lack ability; they disengage because leadership applies the wrong driver. Throughout this book, we have challenged common habits of guessing, reacting, and treating everyone the same. Instead, effective leaders learn to diagnose what truly drives behavior, **Praise, Pay, or Position** and then align their systems, conversations, and decisions with that driver, with clarity and consistency.

When used intentionally, praise reinforces standards and makes performance visible; pay legitimizes value through measurable exchange; and position sustains commitment by turning ambition into structured growth. None of the three works well in isolation. Praise without progression can feel symbolic. Pay without standards can create entitlement. Position without preparation can destabilize teams. But when leaders apply the right motivational driver at the right time and revisit it as people grow, development becomes predictable, retention strengthens, and culture becomes deliberate rather than accidental.

Practical Steps: How to Apply the Three P's Starting This Week

Diagnose the driver (don't assume). Over the next 5-10 workdays, observe what each person repeats, requests, and reacts to. Then confirm it in a short one-on-one by asking:

- What part of your work feels most rewarding right now?
- What would make this role feel like growth over the next 90 days?
- What would make you feel properly valued for the results you deliver?

Decide which driver is dominant right now: Praise, Pay, or Position. Match your response to the driver. If Praise is primary: give specific, timely recognition tied to a standard ("You did X, which produced Y, and that's the level we need."). If Pay is primary: clarify the value exchange; what measurable outcomes justify increased pay, bonus, or incentives. If Position is primary: define the growth path; what readiness looks like, what experiences they need, and what timeline you're working toward.

The P's System

Turn **Praise, Pay or Position** into a system, not a moment. Put structure around what you're doing so it doesn't depend on memory or mood:

1. Praise system: a weekly recognition rhythm (team meeting shout-outs tied to metrics/standards).

2. Pay system: documented performance metrics tied to raises/bonuses and a consistent review cadence.

3. Position system: a visible readiness scorecard and planned developmental assignments (projects, exposure, stretch responsibilities).

Run a 30-day "micro-test."

Make one intentional adjustment based on the driver and watch the response:

- Increase specific recognition - does initiative increase?

- Clarify pay metrics and targets - does focus and output increase?

- Provide a development assignment and readiness milestones -does engagement and commitment increase?

The goal is evidence, not guessing.

Reassess quarterly (drivers can change). Revisit the driver in regular development conversations. As responsibilities and life stages change, what motivates a person can shift. Your leadership stays effective when your diagnosis stays current.

As you return to your team, make this your leadership discipline: stop assuming and start observing. Listen for the language people repeat, watch what they respond to, and hold intentional conversations that reveal what they value most right now. Then lead with precision recognizing what should be repeated, reward what is measurable, and prepare people for what comes next. If you commit to practicing the Three P's consistently, you will not only improve performance, you will build people, strengthen loyalty, and create the kind of workplace where high performers can see a future.

LEADERSHIP APPLICATION GUIDE

The ideas in *The Three P's of People Development* are designed to be applied — not just read.

Leadership development resources help managers accurately diagnose motivation and apply the appropriate driver.

Free Templates, Tools, and Resources

Continue your leadership development journey with practical tools you can use right away.

Free resources include:

- One Page Overview
- Diagnostics
- Conversation Tools
- Recognition and Retention

Or visit: gmgmanagementgroup.net

Leadership Workbooks

Practical companion workbooks are designed to help leaders apply the Three P's of People Development in real-world organizational settings.

Workbooks include:

- Leadership reflection exercises
- Employee motivation diagnostic tools
- Manager coaching templates
- Real-world leadership scenarios
- Action planning

These resources designed for individual leaders, management teams, and leadership development programs.

Manager Playbooks

The Three P's of People Development Manager Playbook Series translates the model into practical tools for daily use by managers.

Playbooks include:

- Performance conversations
- Recognition strategies that drive results
- Retention and engagement tools
- Leadership decision models
- Team development systems

Each playbook is designed to help managers apply the right leadership driver at the right time.

Narrative-Based

Leadership Workshops

Interactive workshops are designed to help leaders apply the Three P's of People Development through real-world leadership scenarios.

Workshops include:

- Narrative-based leadership problem-solving
- Motivation misdiagnosis exercises
- Team retention scenarios
- Leadership decision simulations

Participants work through realistic organizational scenarios and learn how to diagnose whether the issue is related to praise, pay, or position.

Incentive Design Exercises

Many organizations face challenges because incentives do not align with employee motivation.

The Incentive Design Exercise assists leadership teams:

- Assess current reward systems
- Align incentives with key motivational drivers
- Identify gaps in recognition, compensation, or career advancement pathways
- Design performance-based incentive structures

These exercises help organizations avoid the common mistake of using pay to address problems caused by position or recognition gaps.

Leadership Diagnostic Assessments

Structured diagnostic tools have been developed to assist leaders identify the motivational drivers of employee engagement and retention.

Assessments include:

- The Motivation Diagnostic
- Organizational Recognition Assessment
- Leadership Incentive Alignment Assessment
- Team Development Diagnostic

These assessments provide leaders with data-driven insights into what motivates their teams, supporting better decision-making.

Executive Masterclasses

Organizations can participate in the Three P's of People Development Leadership Masterclasses to gain insights to enhance performance and retention.

Masterclasses explore:

- Identifying employee motivational driver
- Aligning praise, pay, and position appropriately
- Avoiding leadership misdiagnosis
- Building performance-driven cultures
- Developing future leaders

Masterclasses are available both online and in person for organizations.

Speaking Engagements

Marvin D. Glover delivers keynotes and leadership workshops focused on practical leadership development and improving organizational performance.

Popular keynote topics include:

- The Three Drivers of People Development
- Why Organizations Misidentify Motivation
- How Leaders Retain High Performers
- Recognition as a Performance Multiplier

Keynotes and workshops are designed for leadership conferences, corporate development programs, executive retreats, organizational leadership initiatives.

Onsite Leadership Development

Organizations interested in implementing the Three P's of People Development model across management teams can request custom on-site leadership development programs.

Programs may include

- Leadership training workshop
- Case-based leadership labs,
- Manager certification programs
- Executive leadership sessions
- Organizational culture development
- Performance management consulting

Connect With GMG Management Group LLC

For information contact GMG Management Group LLC.

Website: gmgmanagementgroup.net

The Three P's of People Development

Great leaders do not guess what motivates people. They diagnose it.

www.ingramcontent.com/pod-product-compliance
Lightning Source LLC
LaVergne TN
LVHW090612110826
845146LV00001B/354

* 9 7 9 8 9 9 5 9 2 3 6 0 2 *